TEN
ADVENTUROUS
WALKS IN
THE SOUTH CHILTERNS

Raymon

GW00685861

Illustra.... ....
Jackie Hei

ISBN 1 874476 05 5

Published by Morning Mist Publications 1994
PO Box 108, Reigate, Surrey RH2 9YP
©Raymond Hugh & Jackie Hei 1994

Designed and Printed by
Advanced Data Graphics, Sevenoaks

INDEX

INTRODUCTION

THE ADVENTURE

The adventure must be yours, it is the thrill of exploration, the pleasure of experiencing something new and the surprise of the unexpected. You could do the same walk several times and each time it will be different. You may spot a tiny muntjac deer grazing in a sun speckled clearing or a squirrel digging to find its winter store. In summer the woods are a myriad of greens, alive with the melody of birdsong and the brisk rustle of leaves as woodland animals forage for the sudden abundance of food. In winter the woods have a forbidding darkness, the trees bare and swaying mournfully in the wind. The leafy foliage gone, animals dart quickly from shadow to shadow whilst birds hunt for food in relative silence. The season can change not only the appearance of walk, but also the feel. The adventure is discovering the secrets of the route on the day.

THE REWARD

The reward is the sense of achievement and the knowledge that not only have you completed a respectable distance, you have learned and experienced something of the Chilterns which before was a mystery. There is no greater satisfaction than to discover the country as our ancestors did - on foot.

WHEN TO GO

Many walkers make the mistake of only walking in fine weather, leaving the hills at the slightest sign of rain. In wet and windy weather the countryside is untamed and with the majority of the population safe in their houses, one can really get a feeling of remoteness and a better idea of what the Chilterns were like several hundred years ago. My suggestion is that you try and do the walks in all seasons and all weathers. At the end, if you don't hate me, you will really begin to feel an affinity with the Chiltern countryside and have the satisfaction of knowing the area well. As for the time of day, I recommend that you try and time your walk to include either dawn or dusk. These to me are the best part of the day, unfortunately, often missed by the majority.

PREPARATION

Planning the walk is as important and enjoyable as doing the walk itself. Firstly, consider whether you want to make a weekend of it. If you do, then I suggest you book local accommodation. This not only cuts down on travelling on the day, but creates a seemingly longer weekend and allows you to remain familiar with the area at night. There is nothing better in my mind, than to finish a long walk and retire to local accommodation for a hot bath before a well earned visit to the local village pub, without having to worry about driving home. A selection of recommended accommodation is listed at the end of each walk.

Once you have decided on your walk, familiarise yourself with it. Read the walk through, following it on the map and ensure you understand where it is you are going. The route descriptions contain points of interest and you may want to take time to stop and visit these. If you do, it might be worth borrowing a book from the library to read up before your visit. Equally, when you have made up your mind on the points of interest to visit, try and estimate the length of your walk. The timings given on each walk are meant as a rough guide only and are based on a person being reasonably fit. If you are unsure, then I suggest you allow for approximately two miles per hour. Timing is important as you could find yourself stumbling back to the start in the dark.

i

Finally, make sure you are fit. The walks in this book are longer than the average walking book and can be hard work if you are unprepared. To help identify the gradients, a cross section is included at the start of each walk.

WHAT TO TAKE

A good map is essential. I recommend you use the Ordnance Survey Landranger maps and the start of each walk details the map(s) required. You can also use the Ordnance Survey Pathfinder maps which have far more detail such as field boundaries, but they can be harder to find and can ultimately be more expensive. The Chiltern Society also publish a number of detailed maps which contain a vast amount of valuable information for the walker.

Once armed with your map, make sure you have sensible clothing. This means clothes which are loose and comfortable. Tight jeans and high heels are not recommended! No matter how good the weather is at the start of the day, always pack some waterproofs. Being caught out in the rain without the necessary protection is not an experience I would recommend. In summer if you are walking in shorts, waterproof trousers are also particularly useful as a temporary protection against nettles. There is a wide range of waterproof clothing now available. The two recommendations I would make are :-

(1) Make sure you are completely covered, that is buy trousers and a jacket.

(2) Buy clothing made from one of the breathable materials - your local stockist will advise you on these.

If the weather is cold, then gloves and a hat are always advisable. No matter what time of year, I always pack a jumper and have never regretted it. Keeping warm helps avoid tiredness. Most importantly, make sure you have a good pair of shoes. If you can afford it, then buy a pair of walking boots. If not, then make sure your shoes are strong, comfortable and have soles with a good grip. Equally important are good socks. If you have boots then two pairs are advisable. Do not think that the socks you wear to the office will do!

Sensibly clothed, you can now think about other equipment you may need. A camera and a pair of binoculars are always useful and can enhance your day out. I always carry a pocket book on birds, you could do the same or add to this with a book on local flora or history. You will find the walk all the more enjoyable for a little bit of knowledge. Do not though, get over enthusiastic and take a library or you may find yourself requiring a book on first aid!

A basic first aid kit however, is always advisable. The Chiltern countryside may appear tame and so it is compared to the Himalayas, but it must still be treated with respect. The book and the map should be enough to find the route without difficulty, however a compass is always useful for finding your way when paths are underfined.

Refreshments are always an important consideration. There are places where you can get a bite to eat on every walk, but even if you wish to use these facilities, it is important to carry some basic snacks, especially in cold weather. You should always / water and a thermos flask with a hot drink or soup can also be very welcome.

To carry everything you need for your walk, I recommend you invest in a comfortable day sack or small rucksack. These are now available from a wide assortment of shops, but before you make your purchase, make sure it is strong and more importantly, that it is comfortable.

Finally, take your five senses with you - these are essential if you are to fully appreciate the walk but, most importantly, **ENSURE YOU TAKE THIS BOOK.**

GETTING THERE

Most people will be mobile, i.e. a car or bicycle. Where practical, I have listed railway stations. Buses however, are far more difficult as their routes and timetables tend to change with the wind. For those people relying on a bus to reach the start, I have listed the main bus companies serving the area.

Buckinghamshire Travel Line (Tel.0296 382000)

Chiltern Bus (Tel.0494 464647)

Chiltern Queens (Tel.0491 680354)

Ridgeway Explorer (Tel.0367 718929)

This service is run by the Regis Bus Company. It is a new venture operating in summer only and is especially designed for walkers. Its future depends entirely on the number of people who use it.

Wycombe Bus Company (Tel.0923 673121)

For information on rail services, telephone :

The Chiltern Line - 071 387 7070

The Henley Line - 071 928 5100

The Thames Valley Line - 071 262 6767

ROUTE FINDING

The route descriptions are instructional rather than poetic and should be followed without difficulty. To assist you, a series of symbols in the left hand margin enable you to identify specific points on the walk at a glance. A good map is essential and should be used in conjunction with the route description. Please remember that like everything else, the countryside changes with time, e.g. a fenced path can become unfenced and vice versa.

Before setting out, make sure you have identified the route on the map. To pinpoint a starting point or place of interest and key points on the route, I have used grid references which are printed in bold in the text. These are six figured numbers which identify a particular point on the map. Every Ordnance Survey map is covered by a national grid. The grid's lines are identified by numbers printed on the map's surround. To find a grid reference, take the first three numbers, which refer to the vertical lines on your map and locate them on the top or bottom (north or south) of the map. The third number is an imaginary line in the square following the first two numbers. To find this line, divide the square into ten equal parts. Then take the last three numbers, which refer to the horizontal lines and locate them on the left or right (east or west) of your map and follow the line of this reference until it meets the line of the first reference. Their meeting point is the grid reference point itself. Do not rely on the maps in this book, these are not to scale and are designed as a rough guide only.

It is important that you recognise the various types of footpath signs. Most are fairly obvious, i.e. wooden post with a sign marked 'footpath' or 'public bridleway', pointing in the direction of the right of way. Some will have the name of a specific route, for example. 'The Ridgeway'.

Over recent years many County Councils have standardised their signs to follow national guidelines. Footpaths are now shown with a yellow arrow and bridleways with a blue one. Like the old wooden signs, the arrows will point in the direction of the right of way. Some arrows will have the name of a recognised walk encircling them, an example is 'The South Bucks Way'. Also, because of the mainly woodland environment of the Chilterns, another form of way marking is the painting of white

arrows on trees. These are invaluable in autumn when the fall covers the paths making them invisible save for the arrows. On top of all this, you will often find custom built signs. These can mark an official route but more often than not are the work of local farmers guiding the walker across their land. An example of the former is 'The Ridgeway' which is highlighted by a white acorn on a black background.

An important rule on route finding is to take your time. Follow the map and read the route description thoroughly. If you do this, then you will return to base without mishap.

LONG DISTANCE WALKS
Many of the routes in this book meet long distance linear walks which run through the Chilterns. In case you want to try any, I have listed their names and distances below, together with the publisher who produces a description of the walk.

Beeches Way - 16 miles (Buckinghamshire County Council)

London Country Way - 205 miles (Constable)

North Bucks Way (leaflet) - 35 miles (Buckinghamshire County Council)

Oxfordshire Way - 65 miles (Oxfordshire County Council)

Ridgeway Path - 85 miles (Aurum Press)

South Bucks Way (leaflet) - 23 miles (Buckinghamshire County Council)

Swans Way (leaflet) - 65 miles (Buckinghamshire County Council)

Thames Path - 156 miles (Ramblers Association)

Thames Valley Heritage Walk - 107 miles (Constable)

TOURIST INFORMATION CENTRES
If you require any further information on transport, tourist facilities or accommodation, I have listed the local Tourist Information Centres over the page.

Henley on Thames - Tel.04391 578034

High Wycombe - Tel.0494 421892

Marlow - Tel.0628 483597

Walllingford - Tel.0491 35351

Wendover - Tel.0296 623056

PROTECTING THE CHILTERNS

The special beauty of the Chilterns is protected by a number of organisations. Apart from protecting and managing the environment, they also organise a variety of activities and events throughout the year.

Supporting these organisations will ensure their survival and the continued protection of a landscape threatened by urbanisation. I have listed below the organisations which deserve special praise I've listed below along with a telephone number or address from where you can obtain membership details.

BBONT - local wildlife trust - Tel.0865 775476

Chiltern Society - P.O. Box 1029, Marlow, SL7 2HZ

National Trust - P.O.Box 39, Bromley, Kent, BR1 1NH

Woodland Trust - Tel.0476 74297

AUTHOR'S NOTE

Every effort has been made to ensure that the route descriptions are accurate. Time changes things however, and can alter the description of the route. If you have any difficulty in finding any part of a route, please write with details giving a grid reference, to enable me to re-examine the route. A free copy of the next publication will be forwarded for any suggestions used in the next edition. Enjoy your walks.

TAMING THE LIONS

Distance: 9½ miles (15.25 km)

Time: Allow approximately 5 hours

Map: Ordnance Survey Landranger Map 165

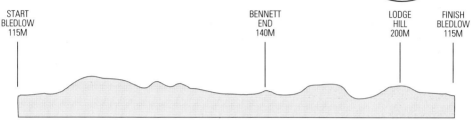

| START BLEDLOW 115M | BENNETT END 140M | LODGE HILL 200M | FINISH BLEDLOW 115M |

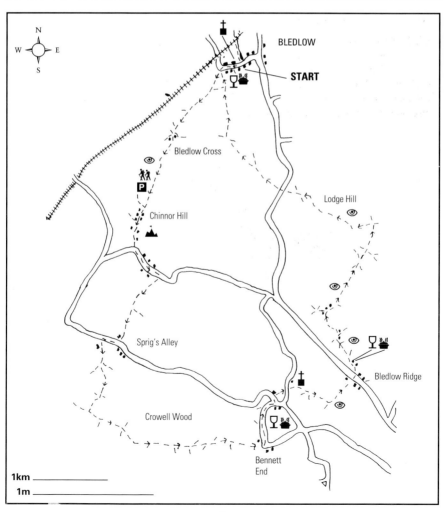

Walk Summary

This beautiful walk enables you to tame the wild and beautiful scenery around Chinnor Hill and Bledlow Ridge. After climbing Chinnor Hill and enjoying some magnificent views across the Vale of Aylesbury, the walk takes you in and out of several wooded valleys, before following the old Oxford to London coaching route to Bennett End. After Bennett End, the route traverses a countryside of high ridges and steep valleys, with glorious views in virtually every direction. The final stretch leads over Lodge Hill, with more superb views before returning to Bledlow.

There is hardly a dull moment on this walk and even though there are many ups and downs, the scenery enables you to forget any aches and pains. If for some amazing reason it doesn't, there are some excellent hostelries en route to help! If you time the walk carefully to end at Lodge Hill at dusk, you may be rewarded with a magnificent sunset over the Vale of Aylesbury. Doing this in summer would mean starting at "The Lions of Bledlow" pub at lunchtime and finishing during opening hours in the evening, an excellent way to start and finish, though the lions would be in danger of taming you as opposed to the other way around! One word of warning in this enthusiastic summary, I must mention that after Chinnor Hill there is a short stretch of road walking. This can, at times, be quite busy for a country road and if you have children or a dog, they should be kept under close control.

Start - OS. 777022 Map 165

The walk starts from the church at Bledlow village where there is road parking beside the church itself. If there is a service in progress, then parking can be found a little further on, near the pub, "The Lions of Bledlow". To get to Bledlow, take the B4009 in between Princes Risborough and Chinnor (from the M40 the B4009 can be joined at junction 6), and on reaching Bledlow, marked as Pitch Green on the Ordnance Survey map, turn into Perry Lane, signposted to Bledlow Ridge and Wycombe. Follow the lane under a railway bridge and shortly after, turn right into Church End. The church is a little way up on the right.

An alternative start can be made from a car park at the top of Chinnor Hill (**OS. 767006**), though unless you are local this is quite hard to find. The nearest railway station is at Princes Risborough from where you can join the walk by following a beautiful footpath through the hamlet of Horsenden to Bledlow.

TAMING THE LIONS

Starting from Bledlow, you are starting from one of the prettiest and most historic villages in the Chilterns.

Bledlow (OS. 777022 Map 165) *is situated between the Lower and Upper Icknield Way, two prehistoric tracks with the Upper Icknield Way reputedly being the oldest road in Europe.. The Upper Icknield Way follows the spring-line along the Chiltern escarpment and in later years when the risk of attack lessened, people left the protection of hill forts to form villages around these springs. This happened at Bledlow.*

There is much evidence of prehistoric and Celtic settlements in the area but Bledlow is essentially a Saxon village. There is some argument over the origin of the village's name, the name is certainly Saxon but can be interpreted as "the place of a burial of a Saxon called Bledda" or "bloody hill", referring to a battle between the Saxons and the Danes which took place on the hill overlooking the village. The hill, now called Wains Hill, has a turf cross cut into its side and our route later passes just below it when we will learn more.

Bledlow Church

The layout of the village is as it would have been in Saxon times with the church sited on the spring-line. The spring at Bledlow is undoubtedly the most dramatic in the Chilterns. Water tumbles straight out of the hillside into a lush ravine beside the church, to form the Lyde Brook. The spring is so strong that it once supported a paper mill, built only tens of metres from the source. Further down the hill, it also supported watercress beds. The source is now the feature of an attractive garden, the Lyde Garden, which is open to the public. The garden has been cleverly designed with raised wooden walkways taking the visitor above pools of crystal clear water, surrounded by rich vegetation. It was a gift to the village from the Carrington family who own the manor house opposite the garden entrance. The entrance is discreet and therefore, quite hard to find. To assist, it is accessed via a low gate from the road and to the right of the church. From the garden, the water appears to gush from beneath the church and has led over the years to speculation that the church may at any time collapse. This has led to a local rhyme.

"They that live and do abide,
Shall see the church fall in the Lyde."

The church which dates from Norman times, continues to make a mockery of the rhyme and its author. Unfortunately, the church which has remained virtually unaltered on the outside since the 13th century, is nearly always locked. A footpath through the churchyard to the right of the church, affords probably the best views of the Lyde spring and the ravine and further on, it passes the old paper mill.

The manor house which dates from the 18th century, was sold to Lord Carrington in 1801. Once or twice a year the Carrington family throw open the doors to the public. For details, contact the Tourist Information Centre at Wendover.

The rest of the village is a mixture of period cottages, some dating back to the 16th century. There are very few villages today that can boast such a pretty and well preserved collection.

To start the walk, facing the church, turn left to follow the road west passing by pretty cottages and a brick post box. After a short distance, you will arrive at a green in front of the village pub, "The Lions of Bledlow", a free house. The pub was formed from three shepherds' cottages and the three open fires are still in use today. Inside, exposed beams abound and the low light and flickering fires create a distinctly cosy atmosphere. If you look carefully, you can make out the original outline of the three cottages and part of the pub still retains the original tiled floor.

3

The pub serves a good choice of food and compliments it with a range of five real ales. There is a pleasant garden out back, though many people prefer to sit below the pub sign on the green at the front. Not surprisingly, the pub can be very busy at Sunday lunchtimes, but even with the crowds I still believe it to be one of the best pubs in the Chilterns. Miss out on "The Lions" and you will miss out half the walk, though go easy or you could end up like the character on the front cover of this book!

The lane you are on bends right here and you should leave it to follow another lane ahead, passing in front of the pub. Just after the pub, ignore a track left and carry straight on to take a signposted public footpath across the centre of a field, bearing gently left heading for the tree covered Wain Hill. At the far side of the field, turn right onto a track, part of the Swan Way, a sixtyfive mile bridleway. Follow the track as it climbs gently uphill, becoming steeper as you go. As you progress, there are good views behind across the Risborough Gap to Coombe Hill and Cymbelines Castle, featured in The Hampden Howler, another walk in this book. Ignore all turnings off to eventually reach and pass through a gate onto a path in front of a cottage. This is the Upper Icknield Way and also the route of one of Britain's most popular long distance trails, the Ridgeway.

The Upper Icknield Way is reputed to be the oldest road in Europe having been in constant use since the stone age. From the south coast the road passed through Dorset to Stonehenge and then along a chalk ridge (hence the name the Ridgeway), to eventually cross the Thames at Streatley. Thereafter, it continues along the Chiltern escarpment to Grimes Graves in Norfolk (neolithic flint mines), and onto the east coast at The Wash. When the road was in its earliest period the English Channel did not exist and it is probable that from both coastlines it extended to the Continent. This would explain the similarity of the neolithic and bronze age remains in Brittany and those along the Icknield Way. It would also account for the vast amount of trade which the Icknield Way is known to have carried. Successive archeological digs have uncovered goods which have come from as far away as Egypt.

This part of the Upper Icknield Way, close to the Risborough Gap, was a strategically important location. Consequently, there is much evidence of early settlement, particularly during the bronze and iron ages. A bronze age round barrow close to here, known locally as the Cop, when excavated, was found to contain, among other things, a polished axe of greenstone, believed to have come from St. Ives in Cornwall. This is a good example of the distances people would travel to trade.

As mentioned earlier, the Upper Icknield Way followed the spring-line along the Chiltern escarpment, allowing a constant source of fresh water for the traveller. The Lower Icknield Way travels in almost a straight line below the escarpment, some distance from the ancient settlements. It is believed that this was a later road, probably formed by Romano Britons during the Roman occupation. Although not a Roman road, there is evidence in places of surfacing of a type used by the Romans. The most likely explanation is that the Britons continued to use the well established Icknield Way, but with a peaceful occupation by the Romans, created a more direct and easier route along the plain, using techniques learned from the Romans to overcome the difficulties of the muddier stretches.

The name Icknield is thought to be derived from the Celtic Iceni tribe of Norfolk, though many believe that the name is much older than this and could even be the oldest name still in existence today. In later years, the Upper Icknield Way formed part of an old drovers road and one of the cottages here which make up the hamlet of

Hempton Wainhill, was once a drovers ale house called "The Leather Bottle". Some of the gardens stem from the original sheep folds.

Today, it is fitting that the Upper Icknield Way forms part of a long distance trail. Preserved from the ravages of the motor car, walkers can experience Britain in the same way as the Ridgeway's earliest users and hopefully appreciate what so many have forgotten.

Bear right in front of the cottage and after a few paces, ignore a path off to the right and continue on for a few more paces to where the path forks. Take the left hand fork which leads gently uphill and is signposted as a bridleway, thereby leaving the Ridgeway and the Icknield Way. The bridleway climbs the scarp slope of Wain Hill. The name Wain Hill is of Saxon origin and literally means "hill of streams", a very *i* appropriate description considering the number of springs at its base. A little further up, the path runs between fairly steep banks, a sign that this was also an ancient route. To avoid the mud, I advise that instead of following the bridleway between the banks, you take the path which runs along the top of the bank on the right. The steady climb takes you just below the Bledlow Cross.

The Bledlow Cross (OS. 769009 Map 165), *along with the Whiteleaf Cross the* *i* *other side of the Risborough Gap, are the only two turf cut crosses in England. The most popular theory is that they are of neolithic origin, possibly even fertility symbols converted to crosses by early Christians. Another theory is that they were cut to guide travellers along the Icknield Way. Whatever you believe, it is almost certain that the Bledlow Cross is of later origin, possibly even as late as the 17th century.*

Continue to climb, ignoring all turnings off, until you are almost at the top of the hill where you should look out for a narrow path leading off to the right, between two wooden posts. (If you miss it, do not worry as the path rejoins the main bridleway a little further on). Take this, thereby leaving the bridleway, and follow it as it levels off and after a short distance, follows a fence on your right. At the same time, the wood gives way to open hillside which is in fact a nature reserve run by BBONT, who are trying to restore the natural grass downland and encourage the chalkland flowers.

There are a couple of benches here, thoughtfully placed, allowing you to enjoy the magnificent views over the Vale of Aylesbury in comfort. Continue straight on and ◉ immediately after the second bench, fork left to shortly rejoin the bridleway followed earlier. Turn right along the bridleway to re-enter woodland and continue ahead, ignoring all minor turnings off, until you eventually meet a "T" junction just after passing a BBONT nature reserve sign for Chinnor Hill.

Turn left at the "T" junction along a semi-tarmacked lane and almost immediately after, turn right passing through a small parking area (alternative start). Do not pass through a farm gate ahead. After the parking area continue to shortly follow a lane, passing some attractive cottages and houses at the top of Chinnor Hill. It may be re-assuring to know that you have already reached the highest point on the walk. Follow the lane to its end, a "T" junction with another lane, and turn left along the latter, Red Lane, for a few hundred metres (taking care of the traffic), before turning right onto a signposted bridleway, also signposted to Sprig's Alley. This is at the far end of a small wood on your right **(OS. 767994).**

The bridleway which can be extremely muddy in wet weather, at first passes a water tower on your right and continues along the left hand perimeter of the wood with fields on your left. After some distance, it begins to descend and soon after, the fields on your left end. You should continue downhill, ignoring all turnings off, to reach the bottom of the valley where in spring and summer you will be greeted by the pungent smell of ramsons (wild garlic) which cover the floor. Here, the bridleway becomes a track. A few paces on as the track bends sharp left, you should leave it to pass through a gate on your right, signposted as a bridleway (blue arrow), thereby maintaining your route. The bridleway leads up the other side of the valley with the wood now on your left and a field on the right.

At the far side of the valley pass through a small wooden gate and continue ahead along a narrow path, following the perimeter of the grounds of a house on your right. This soon brings you to a lane in front of a beautiful white cottage. Welcome to Sprig's Alley. Do not get too excited by the pub marked on the Ordnance Survey map here as this has now been converted into a restaurant. You will simply have to go thirsty!

Turn right along the lane and after approximately two hundred metres, left onto a concrete drive for "Crowell Hill Farm", also signposted as a public bridleway. A few paces on, leave the drive and take a narrow path which forks left and runs downhill between banks through a wood. The path can often be extremely muddy and difficult to negotiate, even in summer. To avoid the mud, a few paces on, take a narrow path right up the side of the bank and follow it, thereby maintaining your route downhill, running parallel with the sunken bridleway.

Eventually, you will arrive at a crossing path where there is a hollow on your right. You should carry straight on here where after a few paces, arrows on a tree trunk indicate that the route forks. Take the left hand fork, the bridleway, which continues along the perimeter of the wood with a field now on your right (the right hand fork, as a guide, enters the field itself). The bridleway, now more a track, leads up the other side of the valley through magnificent beech woodland, part of Crowell Wood. As before, keep to the main track and ignore all turnings off, taking heed of the arrows marked on tree trunks. If you are in doubt at this point, remember you should be following the perimter of the wood where you can just about see the field through the trees on your right.

Follow the bridleway which later bends right, with the field perimeter still visible through the trees on your right. Soon after this, the field on your right gives way to Crowell Wood and here you should continue ahead walking straight through the wood along a prominent path, as before following the white arrows marked on tree trunks. At the same time the bridleway begins to descend into another valley.

The going can be quite steep in places and care is needed if you are not to make your descent too speedily! As you descend, ignore a crossing track and continue to the bottom of the valley to meet another crossing track, this one marked as bridleway "S87". Turn left here along the track, following it along the bottom of the valley.

i

It may seem incredible today but this was once the main London to Oxford road and at the time, was the lowest pass through the Chilterns. It still acts as the county boundary for Oxfordshire and Buckinghamshire, Buckinghamshire is on your right. Even when the turnpike road was built (the current A40), many people continued to brave the mud of this route to avoid the tolls. The government later found a way to penalise these dodgers by taxing the vehicle instead of the road, the current road tax. Things have now almost turned full circle with the government today considering re-

introducing road tolls on motorways. I wonder what the old toll dodgers would make of this?

Looking around at the steep wooded valley sides you can see how susceptible travellers once were to unscrupulous highwaymen. One highwayman must have come to a sticky end as his ghost is said to haunt the road, looking for unsuspecting victims. Hang onto those rucksacks!

After a short distance, the woodland on your right gives way to fields which in summer are a mass of poppies, a beautiful part of the walk and a great place for spotting wildlife. Stay on the track, ignoring all turnings off, including a marked crossing path sometime later, keeping to the valley bottom to eventually leave the wood. After the wood, the track continues ahead, still following the bottom of the valley, the track now acting as a dividing line between fields. Soon after, ignore another track off to the right, keeping to the track along the valley bottom, lined in places by ancient oaks. Ignore all further turnings off along the way, including marked bridleways and footpaths, to eventually meet a tarmac lane.

Turn right along the lane making for a house in the distance and ignore a signposted bridleway soon after, off to the right. You will eventually arrive at a small green in the midst of a cluster of houses which make up the hamlet of Bennett End. Ignore a bridleway right here and turn left instead along a lane, Horseshoe Road, which leads up the side of the valley. A short distance on, you will see why I led you along the bottom of the valley and did not take one of the turnings off along the way, for here we will arrive at the excellent "Three Horseshoes Inn", a free house established in 1745. The pub has a small garden, set in beautiful surroundings with superb views over the valley. Inside, there is a small snug bar with a flagstone floor and a large open brick fire, still with its old oven. There is also a slightly larger carpeted lounge bar with a log burning stove, as well as a small restaurant area. The pub offers Brakspear's and Flowers ales. If you want to stay longer, then it also offers overnight accommodation.

After "The Three Horseshoes Inn", continue up the lane ignoring a footpath off to the left and later as it begins to descend, ignore another footpath, also off to the left. Soon after, you will arrive at a "T" junction where you should turn left along a lane, Town End Road, and follow it for approximately fifty metres before turning right onto a signposted public footpath. Ahead of you now in the distance, is the tower of Radnage church. Go across a small grass area and then a gravel drive to cross a stile into a field. Walk straight across the field, heading for the church and at the far side go over a stile, cross a lane and join a tarmac drive ahead which leads to the church, dedicated to St. Mary the Virgin.

St. Mary the Virgin (OS. 786979 Map 165) *has one of the most beautiful settings of any church in the Chilterns. It dates from the 12th century and was built on the site of an earlier Saxon church. Inside, on the walls, are the remains of medieval paintings, dating from the 13th century. These have only recently been discovered. In places the walls are also inscribed with religious text from the Georgian period. The font was discovered buried in a nearby field and is probably from the original Saxon church.*

*The name Radnage is Saxon and literally translated means "place of the red oak".
This was probably a large oak, possibly with red markings, which acted as a
boundary point.*

To continue our route, standing at and facing the porch and entrance to the church,
turn right and follow a fairly prominent path through the churchyard, at the far end
of which you will meet an unusual curved stile, built into the churchyard wall. Cross
the stile and then a wooden stile into a field and go diagonally right across the field,
heading for another stile at the far side. Go over the stile into another field and take
care at this point not to take the main path ahead across the field, but bear
diagonally left instead to cut across the left hand corner. You should now be heading
for a stile on the left hand perimeter beside a wood.

Go over the stile and follow the footpath uphill for a few paces before bearing right
to follow a narrow path along the edge of the hill. Soon after, you will arrive at open
grass hillside dotted with anthills. As you meet this the path forks (take care not to
miss it), and you should take the left hand fork which leads uphill along the left
hand edge of the grass clearing. As with many other grass hillsides in the Chilterns,
you are rewarded here in summer with a beautiful display of wild flowers. The
hillside is an ideal place to pause for a rest or for a picnic. The numerous anthills,
made by the yellow ant, are an indication that the hillside has remained
undisturbed for centuries. It is also a sign that if you do stop for a picnic you will
probably be sharing it with some uninvited guests!

The path continues to climb and nearing the top of the hill enters woodland, where
you should cross a stile to follow a path which meanders through the wood. At the
other side, the path bends left and becomes fenced following a line of trees between
fields. If you look carefully in summer, bordering the path wild strawberries can
often be found. There are also excellent views right here of the eastern side of the
valley, along the bottom of which continues the old London to Oxford road.

The route continues uphill, although your climb is much easier now, heading for the
village of Bledlow Ridge. It is not long before the path levels out to soon pass
between houses before meeting a lane. If you turn left here, you will see the
welcome sight of "The Boot" pub, Morland, offering food and an attractive beer
garden, complete with ducks and pond. Our route however, is across the lane to join
a gravel drive the other side, marked as a public footpath. This bends left behind
the pub and continues between houses to soon end where you should carry straight
on along a fenced path. This soon leads to two gates with two stiles. Pass between
the gates to go over the second stile and continue ahead, still following the path
which now runs along the left hand perimeter of a field and is fenced on your right.
As you progress superb views open out to your right across the Risborough Gap to
Windsor Hill and Loosley Row, identified by its windmill.

At the far side of the field, go over a stile and continue to follow the path ahead
which now runs between a bank of trees on your left and a wooden fence on your
right. This soon leads out to a tarmac drive which you should cross to then go over a
stile ahead. After the stile, follow a narrow path ahead through a beautiful field of
wild grassland. This leads to the right hand field perimeter where you should
continue ahead, along the perimeter, to reach a stile at the far side. Go over the
stile, down a steep bank and then over another stile to enter a small field. Follow
the right hand perimeter of the field ahead and ignore two gates on your right, to
reach the far right hand corner and a stile.

Go over the stile and follow a prominent path ahead through a small copse, to soon meet a fence on your left which you should follow. Shortly after, go over a second stile to arrive at a narrow tarmac lane, serving a number of houses which make up the hamlet of Rout's Green. Turn right along the lane which soon bends gently left and when it ends, continue ahead along a track, signposted as a public bridleway. After a short distance, go through a gate into a field where you are rewarded with one of the best views on the walk.

Ignore a signposted footpath right at this point and continue straight on along the marked bridleway. You should now be going downhill along the left hand perimeter of a field, at the far side of which you should pass through a gate to continue ahead across the centre of the next field. On a clear day, to your right, you can see the magnificent manor house at Bradenham featured in "The Hell Fire Hike". At the end of the field, pass through a gap in the hedge and join a track to continue your route ahead (do not turn right). After approximately twenty metres, ignore a gap in the hedge on your left and at the same time a bridleway, and carry straight on, following the left hand perimeter of the field you are in, going gently uphill.

At the far side of the field, ignore a signposted footpath right and continue through a gap in the hedge to follow the left hand perimeter of the next field ahead, going over a crossing track to do so. The bridleway gradually bends left, skirting the edge of Lodge Hill and you should continue for some distance and look out for a crossing path further on, just after passing through a gap in a hedgerow. Turn left onto the crossing path which is in fact the Ridgeway and follow it up the side of Lodge Hill. You will soon meet a stile which you should cross to continue following the Ridgeway, marked by white acorns and low stone signs, to reach the summit of Lodge Hill. The summit is a mixture of grasses and chalk scrub, complete with masses of chalkland flowers. There are marvellous views to be enjoyed from this point, a lovely place to stop and enjoy your surroundings before commencing the last stretch of our walk.

There is evidence (visible from the path) that the hill was once an iron age settlement. Excavations have found pottery from the Celtic Belgae tribe who invaded from the south, as well as animal bones, mostly of small horses. The Celts often sacrificed animals to the gods and horses appear to have been of great significance. There is no sign of fortification and it is likely that Lodge Hill was simply a satellite settlement, protected by the larger settlement at the top of Wain Hill. As you admire the views try to imagine the scene all those centuries ago. A cluster of small round wooden huts, tall pillars of smoke rising from their conical roofs. All around are a variety of noisy farm animals, some in pens, and dogs searching among spoil heaps for scraps. A thin line of women are visible in the distance, slowly making their way up the hill after collecting water from a nearby spring. The view, unlike today, is of wild open countryside, much of it wooded. Numerous paths cross the land below, but one much larger than the others winds its way across the Chiltern escarpment carrying a steady stream of traffic. The hill's inhabitants watch the Icknield Way with interest wondering what trade will come their way today.

Returning to the 20th century, follow the path across the summit of the hill, at one point passing through a line of beech trees, (the old boundary of the iron age settlement), and continue, ignoring any turnings off, to reach the north western tip of the hill. If you have taken my advice and have timed this walk to arrive here just efore dusk, you may be lucky enough to catch a beautiful sunset. The path from here descends the side of Lodge Hill, passing through chalk scrub and at the bottom, continues ahead along the left hand perimeter of a field. The Whiteleaf Cross is now easily visible over to your right.

Soon after entering the field, look out for a stile on your left which you should cross to follow a prominent path across the centre of another field. This route is also marked with the white acorn of the Ridgeway. On nearing the field end go over a crossing track and continue to the far side, where you should go over a stile into the next field. Turn diagonally left to follow a prominent path across the left hand corner of the field and pass through a gap in the hedge at the far side. Cross a lane and go over a tall stile the other side to join a path, just to your left, still signposted as the Ridgeway. This takes you into another field where you should follow the left hand perimeter as it rises gently, affording more good views as you progress, over the Chiltern escarpment and the Vale of Aylesbury.

Just before reaching the far side of the field, ignore a stile on your left and continue for a few paces, to go over a second stile on your left into another field. Turn immediately right to follow the right hand perimeter of the field and continue, ignoring a stile on your right as you progress, to follow the field perimeter, still part of the Ridgeway. The field bends gently right and just before reaching the far side, you should bear gently left, thereby leaving the perimeter, to head for a stile near the left hand corner. This is just to the right of a pair of electricity poles.

Go over the stile to arrive at a track, the Upper Icknield Way, onto which you should turn left. Continue for approximately fortyfive paces after which you should turn right onto a signposted bridleway, thereby leaving the Icknield Way. The bridleway leads down the lower slopes of Wain Hill, between fields, and is bordered by trees which in summer offer a welcome shady canopy overhead. Keep to the bridleway and ignore another track off to the left as you continue, to eventually arrive at "The Lions of Bledlow" pub. From here, you can retrace your steps to our starting point, but before doing so I recommend you reward yourself in taming the lions with a well deserved drink!

ACCOMMODATION

The Three Horseshoes, Bennett End. Tel: 0494 483273
On the walk, this must be one of the most attractive places to stay anywhere in the Chilterns. There are three rooms, all of which are en suite and all have glorious views over the countryside.

Youth Hostel, Bradenham YHA, Bradenham. Tel: 0494 56 2929
Approximately three and a half miles from the walk, the hostel is in a converted Victorian school at the edge of the village green. It is only a few minutes walk to the village pub, "The Red Lion", making this an ideal place to stay if you are on a budget.

Camping and Caravanning, Karma Farm, Radnage. Tel: 0494 484136
Approximately half a mile from the walk, this is a Camping and Caravanning Club certified site for members only. (To join, telephone 0203 694886). It is in a beautiful location with fine views and good facilities.

DEFEATING THE DANES

Distance: 10 miles (16 km)

Time: Allow approximately 5 hours

Map: Ordnance Survey Landranger Map 175

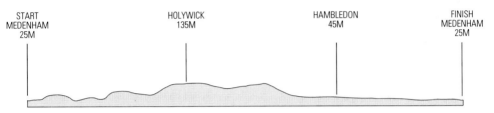

| START MEDENHAM 25M | HOLYWICK 135M | HAMBLEDON 45M | FINISH MEDENHAM 25M |

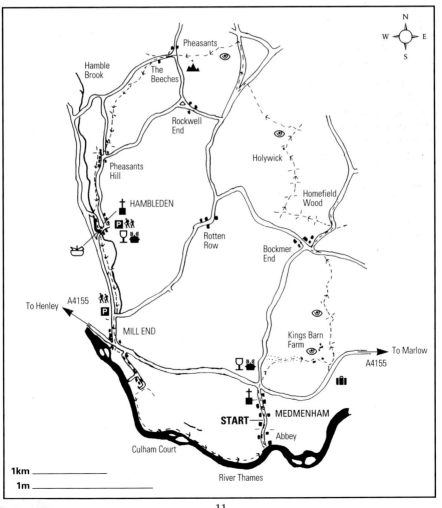

Walk Summary

This is a lovely walk and a good introduction to the Chilterns taking in a wide variety of scenery without being too strenuous. From the Thames-side village of Medmenham the route quickly climbs to cross the patchwork plateau between the Hamble valley and Marlow. It then makes a dramatic descent into the Hamble valley itself before finally following a beautiful and remote stretch of the Thames back to Medmenham. There are several pleasant surprises along the way, including some fine views and two good hostelries. Mud can be a problem in wet weather so do not forget to wear those boots.

Start - OS. 805840 Map 175

The walk starts from Medmenham village. The village basically consists of one narrow lane leading from the A4155 down to the Thames. To get there, take the A4155 and mid-way between Henley and Marlow at Medmenham, turn into Ferry Lane which is beside the village church and almost opposite "The Dog and Badger" pub. There is no car park but road parking is possible virtually anywhere along the lane though as always, please be considerate of the local population.

There are two good alternative starts. One is the Mill End car park just off the A4155 on the road to Hambleden (OS. 784855). The other is the public car park at Hambleden itself. There are railway stations at Henley and Marlow and from both towns it is possible to get a bus to "The Dog and Badger" at Medmenham.

DEFEATING THE DANES

From wherever you have parked, walk back up Ferry Lane to reach the A4155 beside the village church. Standing in the churchyard, facing Ferry Lane, is the village sign depicting a Viking longboat which at once arouses your interest in the village's history.

Medmenham (OS. 805845 Map 175), despite the village sign, is essentially of Celtic origin. The Celts built a fort on a hill above the village, visited shortly on our walk. The Saxons later developed the current layout of the village which during this period, became a small port. The Saxons also built the first church, probably of wood, on the site of the current church. It is also probable that at that time, Medmenham was larger than its neighbours, Marlow and Henley.

Village life during the Saxon period would have been busy and quite dangerous being close to the borders of three powerful tribal kingdoms, Mercia, Wessex and Middle Saxon (now Middlesex), who were continually squabbling over territory. In the 9th century, they were forced to unite against the Danes, who after a number of skirmishes launched a concerted attack along the Thames. Although defeated in several important battles, the Danes never really lost their foothold on the lower Thames-side villages and many of the current place-names in the area originate from or remember this period of history, for example Danesfield and Skirmett. At Medmenham the Danes built another fort nearer the river than the old Celtic fort and now the site of the "Danesfield House Hotel". It was from this and other forts that the Danes launched their invasion inland, using the Thames and its tributaries (such as the Loddon to attack Basing), for fast and easy transportation of troops. For centuries a type of guerrilla warfare ensued before the Danes were eventually forced to flee north. They refused however, to accept defeat and continued to launch attacks along the coast which culminated in a series of fierce battles in the late 10th century between the Danish army, led by Cnut, and the Saxons, led by Edmund "Ironside".

In the early 11th century a truce was reached and England was divided roughly in half, the Danes ruling the north and the Saxons the south. In 1017, Edmund "Ironside" died and Cnut finally became the first and only Danish king of all England and to secure his position, married the mother of his old enemy, "Ironside". The marriage failed to bring peace which only really returned to England after the Norman invasion. The Norman lord, Hugh de Bolebec, was granted the Medmenham estate and to protect against further possible invasions along the Thames, built a castle on the site of the old Celtic hill fort. A deeply religious man, de Bolebec is said to have founded the abbey at Medmenham for the Cistercian brotherhood and built the current church. He later became a monk at his own abbey where he eventually died. The church still retains some of its Norman architecture, though the tower and chancel are 15th century.

There are many fine cottages and period houses straddling Ferry Lane, two worth a mention are the 15th century manor house and the beautiful "Yew Tree Cottage", so-called because of its magnificent sculptured yew hedges. There is also Medmenham Abbey, now a private residence on the river side, though of this we will learn more at the end of the walk. One fine building in which you will probably be very interested is "The Dog and Badger", Whitbread, opposite the church at the other side of the A4155. Reputedly dating from the 14th century, this is a particularly cosy pub which retains its original character. It is usefully positioned allowing you to pluck up some dutch courage for the walk ahead, or to celebrate your finish.

To continue, at the end of Ferry Lane, cross the A4155 and join Bockmer Lane the other side and almost immediately after joining, take a signposted footpath on your right leading uphill through woodland. You are now leaving the flat land of the Thames valley to explore the undulating country of the Chiltern hills. The path leads up to a flat hilltop, covered by beech trees, the site of a Celtic hill fort and later the Norman Bolebec castle. When the hill was fortified there would have been no trees blocking the view and the position would have afforded a commanding panorama over the Thames.

i

Walk straight across the hill following the white arrows on the tree trunks and follow the path to eventually meet a fork. Take the left hand fork to, a few paces on, pass through an old iron kissing gate onto a track. Turn left along the track to shortly reach and cross a driveway and thereafter, follow a narrow path ahead passing through a kissing gate to do so. The path soon leads out onto a narrow tarmac lane onto which you should turn right to walk past the old village school, now a private residence. Continue to pass a number of lovely properties, after which the lane deteriorates and later becomes a track which in turn ends in front of an elegant set of gates. Leave the track here to walk across a small green on your left, in the direction of a white arrow, and join a narrow path the other side which runs between some bushes and a large log.

The path leads downhill following the fencing to a property on your right and later meets a white gate. Here you can enjoy some excellent views left over "Kings Barn Farm" nestling in the valley below. Pass through the gate to arrive at the driveway in front of "Pheasantry Cottage", a very attractive building but perhaps somewhat grand to be called a cottage? Follow the drive downhill to soon meet another drive onto which you should turn right and after approximately fifty metres, take a signposted footpath left going gently uphill through Hog Wood, running parallel with the A4155 on your right.

After a short distance, the path levels out and continues along the side of the hill, following the line of a field on your left. Keep to the path which affords more good views over "Kings Barn Farm" on your left, ignoring any narrow paths leading up the side of the hill on your right. This is a lovely part of the walk, particularly in late spring and summer when a variety of woodland flowers border the path. The path eventually breaks free of the wood to come out at an area of newly planted trees. At the time of writing, a lone branchless trunk of a long dead tree stands defiant on the hillside. It is riddled with holes, the larger ones being the work of woodpeckers.

The path descends at this point to meet a crossing track at the bottom of the valley. Go over the crossing track and cross a stile the other side, to continue ahead along the right hand perimeter of a field and up the other side of the valley. At the far right hand corner of the field you will meet a stile which you should cross into Widefield Wood, though first I recommend you take a breather and take your last look back over "Kings Barn Farm". After the stile, follow a prominent path which at first runs along the edge of the wood, before bearing left across its centre. Ignore all turnings off and crossing paths keeping to the main path at all times which is well marked by white arrows. Later, the path passes through an area of densely growing laurels before eventually coming out at a farm drive. Cross the drive and go over a stile the other side and then proceed diagonally right across the centre of a field, to cross another stile at the far right hand corner onto a lane **(OS. 813862).**

Turn left along the lane passing "Widefield" house and after approximately one hundred metres, as you approach the farm buildings of Bockmer End, turn right onto another lane. This at first passes to the right of the farm buildings before continuing between fields. It soon starts to descend and later runs alongside Homefield Wood on your left. Further on, you should ignore a signposted footpath on your right and continue along the lane (which now bends left) for a few metres more to join a signposted footpath on your left, which starts beside a Forestry Commission sign for Homefield Wood.

Pass through a gap beside two gates and continue ahead along a track which runs in a straight line through the wood. The track cuts a wide line through the wood and in summer the space created is often used to its advantage by brightly coloured dragonflies. Eventually, you will meet a track leading off to the right where a white arrow also indicates a footpath off to the left. You should ignore both and remain on the main track to continue ahead.

Sometime on, you will meet another set of white arrows on a tree trunk which mark a crossing path and a few paces on you will actually arrive at the crossing path itself, onto which you should turn right (take care not to miss it). This is a narrow path which initially runs along the top of a bank through the heart of the wood and then later as it starts to climb, continues between banks. Further up, go over a wide crossing track and carry straight on, still going uphill. The path now meanders up the wooded hillside to eventually arrive at another crossing track. As before, you should ignore this and carry straight on, now following the line of a fence on your left.

Eventually, you will reach a stile which marks the perimeter of the wood. Go over the stile, across a grass track and enter a field the other side, where you should continue ahead along the left hand field perimeter. There are good views right now across to "Woodend Farm". At the far side of the field, pass through a gate into the next field and continue in the same direction, again following the field perimeter. As you near the far side of the field, you will come upon a small area of rough ground covered by shrub and the remains of some old farm buildings. This is reputed to be the site of the lost hamlet of Holywick.

Holywick (OS. 808876 Map 175). *The small area of rough ground, a couple of* *shrub covered pits and a few crumbling walls are the only visible clues that there was once a small hamlet here. In fact, if it was not for the name and some ancient documents indicating that a 13th century chapel once stood at Holywick, the visible signs on the ground would probably be passed off as recent farm workings. Loosely translated from old English or Saxon, Holywick means "holy farm or dwelling". This would indicate that Holywick was once a manorial farm with its own chapel, serving a cluster of farm workers' cottages.*

i

There are several possible reasons why the farm and hamlet were abandoned. The single most common reason throughout England was the black death, but this was rare in the Chilterns. Far more likely is that the farm was abandoned for economic reasons. The few crumbling walls incidentally, are not from the original buildings but from recent farm buildings, probably built from materials left over from the abandoned hamlet. Standing here, I tried to imagine what the scene would have been like seven hundred years ago when the hamlet was thriving, but with only windswept fields for company I found it virtually impossible.

Continue to pass the crumbling walls of Holywick and immediately after, turn right onto a crossing path to cut across the corner of the field through which you have been walking. Go over a stile and follow a prominent path across the centre of the next field.

At the far corner of the field, pass through a gap in the hedge to reach a track onto which you should turn left, ignoring at the same time, a footpath which continues ahead. The track initially follows the field perimeter and then bends right to act as a dividing line between fields, where there are lovely views ahead to your left to the hamlet of Rockwell End. The large wood on your left is Heath Wood, a continuation of Homefield Wood through which we passed earlier. As the track enters another field and at the same time bends left, you should leave it to carry straight on along the right hand field perimeter **(OS. 807879).** Take care not to miss this or else you may find yourself having to retrace your steps uphill to join the correct route.

At the far side of the field, go over a stile into another field where you should bear very gently diagonally right across the centre. As a guide, you should head for the right hand corner of a copse/wood directly ahead. As you continue it is worth pausing to look back, where in the distance you can see the twin hilltops of Bowsey and Ashley Hills, the other side of the Thames. Beyond these, in view on a clear day, are the Finchampstead Ridges.

Pass to the right of the copse/wood and continue ahead, heading for a footpath sign, its pole ringed in white. At the far side of the field, go down some steps to meet a lane onto which you should turn left, going downhill to the bottom of a valley. At the bottom, you will meet another lane joining from the right beside a small triangular green. Turn right here to join it, almost going back on yourself, now following the valley bottom. Shortly after, ignore a track off to the left and continue along the lane for approximately half a mile, until you see a signposted footpath on your left, which you should take. This is just after a copse that borders the lane on your left.

The footpath, at first, runs along the perimeter of the copse to soon meet a stile which you should cross into a field. Continue ahead along the right hand perimeter of the field where again there are good views left across into Berkshire. At the far side, go over another stile and follow a narrow path ahead through Bushes Wood. The wood is beautiful at any time of year but in spring it is probably at its best when the floor is a carpet of bluebells. At the far side of the wood, join a track ahead to walk between fields and shortly reach a lane at the hamlet of Pheasants, beside a red telephone box (OS. 794888). At 156 metres, Pheasants also marks the highest point on the walk.

Cross the lane to follow another lane ahead, signposted to Colstrope. At first you will pass a couple of pretty cottages and then a pond where you should ignore a signposted footpath right. Continue along the lane to soon pass "The Beeches" farm (ignore another signposted footpath on the right), and just after the farm as the lane begins to descend, go over a stile beside a gate on your left to join a signposted public footpath. The footpath leads steadily downhill through some lovely beech woodland. It is well used and marked by regular white arrows making it easy to follow. Later, the path gradually bends left and levels out to run along the side of the hill and where gaps in the trees allow, you are afforded some lovely views to your right over the Hamble valley.

The path soon begins to descend once more and later forks. You should take the left hand fork, the higher route, in the direction of a white arrow to follow a path which runs along the top of the valley side. The path continues on a level course for some distance, again with the occasional good view right, before eventually meeting a crossing track marked by white arrows. Go over the crossing track, thereby maintaining your route ahead and keeping to the path, which eventually begins its descent of the valley side. At the same time, the path forks and you should take the right hand fork in the direction of the white arrows, maintaining a steady descent to eventually come out at a lane at the hamlet of Pheasants Hill.

Cross the lane and join a signposted footpath the other side (part of "The Great Skirmett Skirmish"), by going down some steps and following a narrow path between gardens to arrive at a crossing track. Go over the crossing track and continue ahead along a tarmac drive in the direction of a white arrow on an electricity pole and after a few metres as the drive arrives at two relatively modern houses, turn left onto a crossing path, signposted as a public footpath. The path at first runs between gardens and then after passing through a kissing gate, continues in the same direction along the left hand perimeter of a field. There are lovely views right here across the Hamble valley and the Hamble Brook.

At the far side of the field, go over a stile, pass through a narrow strip of woodland and then a kissing gate to enter another field. As before, you should continue ahead heading for a kissing gate at the far side. The valley bottom as you progress, has now levelled out and to your left the first houses of Hambleden come into view. Pass through the kissing gate at the end of the field, and continue ahead along a well defined path through the next field, bearing gently right, to eventually reach another kissing gate beside a footpath sign.

Go through the kissing gate to meet a lane onto which you should turn left. The lane leads you into Hambleden village, passing to the right of the village church and soon after, left of the old bakery, now a gallery reached by crossing the lovely Hamble Brook. After this, the lane bends left to reach the village centre, marked by an old village pump beneath a chestnut tree. There is a village stores on your right should you need to stop for some provisions. If however, you prefer a more hearty stop, then continue ahead and follow the perimeter of the churchyard to reach "The Stag and Huntsman" pub, a free house. For a detailed history of Hambleden, see "The Great Skirmett Skirmish".

Our route as we arrive at the village centre is right along the lane which passes in front of the village stores. The lane soon crosses the Hamble Brook and immediately after this, you should take a signposted footpath on your left by passing through a kissing gate into a field (**OS. 784865**). Continue straight ahead across the centre of a field, in the direction of the footpath sign (do not make the mistake of wandering left following the Hamble Brook), running parallel with the road on your right. As you progress, you will enjoy some lovely views left of the old rectory, now known as "Kenricks" after its builder.

At the far side of the field, go over a stile to the right of a charming brick and flint bridge over the Hamble Brook, to reach a track. Turn right along the track for a couple of paces and then left over another stile into a field. First though, I recommend you take a couple of moments on the bridge to look back at Hambleden. Once in the field, carry on in the same direction, along a grass track which continues to run parallel with the road on your right. At the far right hand corner, pass through a kissing gate onto a lane. Unless you started at the Mill End car park which is on your right, cross the lane and follow a road ahead, in the direction of the signpost for Henley and Marlow.

Follow the road until you reach a "T" junction in the form of the busy A4155 at Mill End. A short detour right here along the A4155 and then across it to follow a signposted footpath the other side, beside the entrance to Hambleden Marina, will take you to the beautiful Hambleden Mill and its famous weir. You will have to retrace your steps to rejoin our walk.

Our route from the "T" junction however, is left along the A4155 in the direction of the sign for Marlow and Bourne End. When the pavement ends after a barn, cross the road and join a track the other side, passing to the left of a house. The track leads through a private parking area for "Mill End Cottages". Although well used, the way through the car park is not a public highway. The permissive route is to continue along the A4155 for a short distance further to take the first lane on the right. The choice is yours, but I feel the road route which has no pavement, can be extremely dangerous, especially if you have young children or a dog.

After the parking area for "Mill End Cottages", the track bends left to pass through another parking area. Continue to follow it round through the second parking area, at the other side of which you should follow a narrow path ahead to soon meet a narrow lane. Join the lane and follow it ahead walking between some pleasant meadows where over to your right, the river Thames is just visible.

The Lost Roman Villa (OS. 786848 Map 175). *Buried beneath the meadow on your right and stretching back to Mill End, are the remains of a Roman villa, the largest in the area, built on the site of a Celtic settlement. Like the Celtic settlement it* *was built as a port, mainly to transport grain grown in the Hamble valley along the Thames to London. Excavation of the villa uncovered skeletons of approximately one hundred infants. The cause of death is unclear though there are a number of possibilities. As still happens in a few third world countries today, it was not unknown for a Roman family to kill their newly born child if it was a girl and although a civilised society for its day, worshipping Roman gods reputedly involved killing an infant as a sacrifice. Skeletons of infants have been discovered in excavations of Roman sites all over England, but not in the quantity found at Mill End.*

Keep to the lane, ignoring all turnings off, until it bends right just in front of two fields. Leave it here and pass through a gate ahead into the field on your right (do not make the mistake of crossing a stile ahead into the field on your left). Immediately after, turn right to follow the perimeter of the field.

The field ends at the bank of the river Thames where you should turn left to follow the Thames down river. As you near the far end of the field, look out for a large brick manor house the other side of the Thames. This is "Culham Court".

i **Culham Court (OS. 789838 Map 175)** *sits majestically above the Thames. The house dates from the 18th century and was restored in the 1930's. A famous tale from the house concerns George III, who whilst dining here insisted on having hot rolls from his favourite baker in London. The only method by which this could be achieved, was to wrap the rolls in hot flannels and transport them by horse.*

On reaching the corner of the field, there is also a lovely view left up the Hamble valley, the white building in the distance is Turville windmill, famous for its appearance in the film "Chitty Chitty Bang Bang". Pass through a gate at the corner of the field and continue ahead, still following the river bank. The large white building ahead of you in the distance is "Danesfield House", a smart hotel built on the site of the Danish fort at Medmenham. On reaching the far side of this field, go over a stile and as before, carry straight on along the river bank where apart from the Thames itself, you are now afforded good views left to "Lodge Farm" perched on a hilltop above "The Dog and Badger" pub, an indication that it is now not far to the finish. The wooded hill to the right of the farm is the iron age hill fort we encountered at the beginning of the walk.

The crossing of this particular field takes some time as it has recently been merged with another to form one long field. Eventually, on reaching the field end, pass through a gate and follow a distinct path ahead to shortly reach a stone monument.

The Medmenham Ferry Monument (OS. 806837 Map 175). *A plaque states "The monument was erected to commemorate the successful action fought by Hudson Ewebank Kearley, First Viscount of Devonport PC, which resulted in a Court of Appeal deciding on 28th March, 1899 that Medmenham Ferry is public". The case arose after a local man, John Weyman, was obstructed by Hudson from carrying*

18

bricks across the river at Medmenham. After going to appeal the judge ruled that the Medmenham ferry route and the bank on either side of the river was a public highway and should be maintained as such. Unfortunately, the ferry has long since ceased to operate.

At the base of the monument is a stone seat where you can take a final rest and enjoy your surroundings. In view and just visible on the same side of the river, is what appears to be a house built around a ruin. This is "Medmenham Abbey".

Medmenham Abbey (OS. 806837 Map 175). *The house is in fact Elizabethan and*   **i** *the ruin a clever folly. The mock ruin is of the old abbey tower and was probably built by the notorious Sir Francis Dashwood, who purchased the house in the mid-18th century. The tower and house create a clever illusion, probably because their builders had the advantage of using materials from the original abbey. The house became infamous as the headquarters and meeting place of Sir Francis Dashwood's Hell Fire Club, whose members were called The Monks of Medmenham.*

The club had fortyfive members, all close friends of Sir Francis and many of them Members of Parliament, including the Lord Mayor of London, the first Lord of the Admiralty and the Treasurer for Ireland. Members of the club specialised in holding outrageous parties, better described as orgies. Twice a year the club held what they called "full meetings", which were basically parties that lasted a week. On these occasions, it is said that members dressed up as monks and introduced ladies, dressed as nuns, who had to be of "a cheerful, lively disposition", to the group. All the ladies had to wear masks. The most memorable moments of these parties, Sir Francis had sculptured in stone and displayed along the river frontage of the house, much to the annoyance of the local population.

The club held its meetings at Medmenham until 1763 when Sir Francis decided to move the club's activities to some spectacular caves beneath a hill at West Wycombe (see "The Hell Fire Hike"). Today, all is peaceful at Medmenham and all signs of the Hell Fire Club, even stone ones, are gone.

To finish, walk past the monument and go over a wooden bridge after which you should continue ahead along Ferry Lane to arrive back at the point from which you started.

ACCOMMODATION
The Stag and Huntsman, Hambleden. Tel: 0491 571227
See "The Great Skirmett Skirmish".

Little Parmoor Farm, Pheasants. Tel: 0494 881600
Virtually on the walk, accommodation is in a delightful and unspoilt 16th century brick and flint farmhouse. Ideal if you like traditional surroundings and a little peace and quiet.

Youth Hostel, Jordans YHA, Jordans. Tel: 0494 873135
Approximately twelve miles from the walk, this is one of my favourite hostels. A wooden building set in two acres of woodland, it has a path leading down to the historic Mayflower barn and a Quaker guesthouse where you can buy a hearty breakfast.

Camping and Caravanning, Swiss Farm, Henley. Tel: 0491 573419
Approximately one and a half miles from the walk, this is a fairly large and busy site close to the Thames.

THE GREAT SKIRMETT SKIRMISH

Distance: 10 miles (16 km)

Time: Allow approximately 5 hours

Map: Ordnance Survey Landranger Map 175

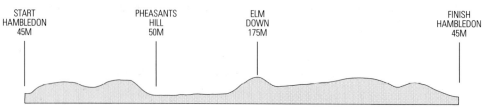

| START HAMBLEDON 45M | PHEASANTS HILL 50M | ELM DOWN 175M | FINISH HAMBLEDON 45M |

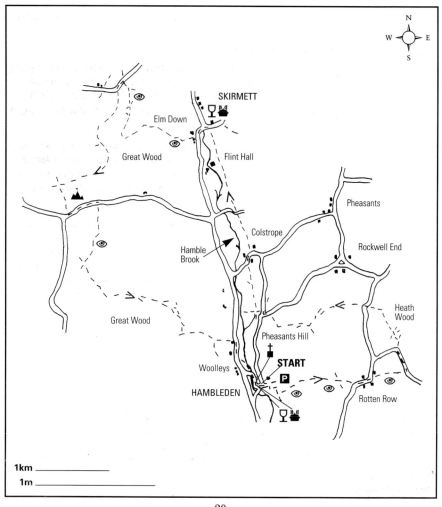

Walk Summary

The Great Skirmett Skirmish explores both sides of the beautiful Hamble valley. After a long excursion into the hills to the east of the valley, the route follows the valley floor to Skirmett, after which it takes to the wooded hills to the west before finally descending to the finish at Hambleden village and the excellent "Stag and Huntsman" pub. Along the way you are rewarded with a rich variety of scenery and some lovely views. The icing on the cake comes in the form of two excellent hostelries en route, as good as any you will find in the Chilterns. There are several steep climbs and the going in places can be very muddy, even in summer, so do not go unprepared.

Start - OS. 785866 Map 175

The walk starts from the public car park at Hambleden village. To get there, take the A4155 in between Marlow and Henley and at Mill End take the road north, signposted to Hambleden and Fingest. After approximately one mile, turn right into Hambleden village and follow the road past "The Stag and Huntsman" pub, to reach the public car park.

The nearest railway station is at Henley on Thames. There is no obvious alternative start.

THE GREAT SKIRMETT SKIRMISH

Having driven through the picturesque Hambleden village to get here, it is tempting to take a stroll around the village lanes before you start. This option is up to you. However, the walk finishes by passing through the village and therefore, I felt it better to detail the village's history at the end when you can enjoy it whilst having a well deserved drink at "The Stag and Huntsman".

From the car park go through a small iron gate which leads onto the village sports field (cricket in summer and football in winter) and turn immediately left to follow the perimeter of the sports field. There are lovely views right here over the Hamble valley to the river Thames and to your left, across to the village's Jacobean manor house, identified by a dome on the roof.

P

◎

"The Manor House" (OS. 785867 Map 175)*, built in 1604, is better viewed from the village centre at the end of the walk. (Please note, that it is private property and not open to the public). It has over the years, had some notable guests and residents. On April 28th, 1646 King Charles I stayed here whilst fleeing to St. Albans after the last of his field armies had been defeated at Stow on the Wold a month earlier. Charles I was finally executed in 1649, "a cruel necessity" according to Cromwell. Coincidentally, one of the signatories on Charles' Order of Execution was Adrian Scrope who was born in the parish.*

i

In 1797 "The Manor House" saw the birth of James Thomas Bradnell, better known as the 7th Earl of Cardigan. He became an M.P. before buying himself the position of Lieutenant Colonel in the 15th Hussars. After falling out with his fellow officers he left to later take command of the 11th Hussars. His fiery temper resulted in a dual with one of his officers and he escaped prison only on a legal technicality. Despite his hot-head reputation, he was appointed Major General in 1847 and in 1854 was sent to the Crimea to command the Light Cavalry Brigade. The Earl suffered from the bitter cold of the Crimean winter and had a woollen jacket specially made to keep him warm, whilst at the same time giving him ease of movement and flexibility. The idea caught on and the garment became and still is known as a cardigan, after the Earl.

Unfortunately, for his men, Cardigan's battle sense was less practical and at the battle of Balaclava he gave a command which was to destroy his regiment. The action is now well known as the Charge of the Light Brigade and sadly was commemorated in perhaps Tennyson's most famous poem. Despite this folly the British went on to win the battle and incredibly, the Earl was welcomed home as a hero. As a reward, he was appointed Inspector General of the Cavalry. It was only later through the word of disillusioned soldiers and historians that the event became recognised as one of the biggest disasters in British military history.

The current residents of "The Manor House" are the family of Viscount Hambleden, descendants of William Henry Smith, the founder of the famous stationery chain, W.H. Smith. His son, also William Henry, entered Parliament in 1868 and on his death as a reward for his services, his widow was made First Viscountess of Hambleden. In 1871, W.H. Smith purchased the Hambleden estate and it is primarily the Viscounts Hambleden that we must thank for preserving the village as we find it today. You can pay your respects to W.H. Smith, M.P., by visiting his grave in Hambleden churchyard at the end of the walk.

Follow the perimeter of the sports field round until you reach an old iron kissing gate on the left. Pass through the gate to arrive at a track and turn left along it for approximately five paces and then turn right to follow a narrow fenced footpath along the edge of a field, going gently uphill.

The going can be fairly tough particularly during the summer months when the path can become overgrown. The views to your right as you progress however, over the Hamble and Thames valleys, are more than worth it. The large brick house visible in the distance the other side of the river Thames, is "Culham Court", an 18th century mansion often visited by George III. After a short distance, the field on your right ends and here you should take one last look back over the Hamble valley before following the footpath uphill through typical Chiltern woodland. The path soon leads out to a large clearing which in summer is a beautiful mass of thistles and wild flowers.

Continue along the footpath where soon after you should cross a track (this has only recently been created for tree-felling and could easily disappear in the future), and a few paces on meet a second track onto which you should turn left, in the direction of a footpath arrow. As a guide, you should still be walking uphill. After approximately fortyfive paces, leave the track to take a footpath right marked by a white arrow on a tree trunk, to shortly meet a stile. Go over the stile into a field and carry straight on along the left hand perimeter. As the field perimeter bends left, you should leave it and bear diagonally right across the centre of the field, still in the direction of the white footpath arrows.

At the far side of the field, pass through a gap in the sparse hedgerow and continue ahead along the left hand perimeter of the next field to soon meet a double farm gate. Pass through the gate and go over a track to follow a grass track ahead which acts as a dividing line between fields. Ahead to your left now, is the farming hamlet of Rotten Row and to your right the wooded hill top of Bowsey Hill in Berkshire.

Stay on the track to eventually meet a lane **(OS. 797866)**. Follow the lane ahead (do not turn right), to soon arrive at Rotten Row, a typical Chiltern hamlet dotted with flint and half timbered cottages and graced by a magnificent farmhouse. Follow the lane through the hamlet and shortly after passing a pond on your righ lane bends left, leave the lane and carry straight on along a concrete drive. This soon leads to a gate through which you should pass to enter a field.

Go across the centre of the field in the direction of a public footpath sign and at the far side, go over a stile into another field and continue in the same direction. On nearing the far side, head for a stile beside a gate and go over this to follow a narrow footpath through woodland. This soon meets yet another stile which you should cross to meet a lane. Turn left along the lane which follows the perimeter of Heath Wood and stay on the lane until it bends sharp left. Here, leave the lane and join a signposted public footpath to continue ahead. This initially takes the form of a tarmac chip parking area for Forestry Commission vehicles.

Continue ahead and keep your eyes peeled for a white arrow painted on the trunk of a tree, also marked with the number "7", on your right. When you spot this, take a narrow footpath right which leads downhill through Heath Wood. The going here is quite dense, a mixture of beech and firs. As the footpath begins to climb again it also forks and you should take the left hand fork, the less prominent route, still marked by white footpath arrows.

Sometime on, go over a crossing path and continue until the woodland ends where you will arrive at a wide crossing track. Go over the crossing track and pass over a stile into a field where you should bear gently diagonally right to follow a prominent path across the field. Just before reaching the far side, follow the left hand field perimeter to shortly reach a stile, topped by white posts. Cross the stile to once again enter Heath Wood and continue ahead, passing a now disused stile, following a path along the perimeter of the wood. As before, to guide your way, there are white arrows painted on the tree trunks.

After a short distance, cross two stiles on your left to enter a field and continue ahead along the right hand perimeter. If you are walking this way at dawn or dusk, then your route will be interspersed by rabbits darting for cover. The field perimeter curves gently right and just before this ends, you should leave it and turn left to follow a distinct path across the centre of the field. You should now be heading for a stile and footpath sign the other side.

Go over the stile mentioned and cross a lane to go over another stile the other side, slightly to your right. You should now follow a track which leads through a strip of beech woodland, where after a short distance you should ignore a signposted footpath off to the right. Continue ahead to later meet a wider expanse of woodland, where your route bears gently left to start your descent of Pheasant's Hill. Shortly after, you will join a track coming in from the right along which you should continue ahead. After approximately fifty metres another track joins from the right and at the same point, a tree on your right is marked with several white arrows. You should ignore all turnings off here and continue straight on along the track you have been following.

After a short distance, you will meet a turning right, again marked by a white arrow. This time, you should leave the track and take the marked footpath right. If you find yourself following a track between fields, then you will have gone too far and should retrace your steps. The footpath, although narrow, is fairly prominent and winds down the side of Pheasant's Hill, with clear views across the Hamble valley. Half way down the hill, ignore a crossing path to continue your descent, taking time to look around you, especially in summer, when the ground is a c   et of wild flowers.

After the crossing path, the footpath continues a long route down the side of Pheasant's Hill. Despite its name, I have never seen a pheasant on the hill - perhaps you will have more luck! Near the bottom of the hill, ignore a now disused stile on your right to shortly after meet a second stile ahead, which you should cross to join a fenced path between fields. The hamlet of Pheasant's Hill, our next destination, is now in view. At the far side of the fields, the footpath twists left to follow the perimeter of a garden on your right and shortly meets a lane in front of a pretty flint and brick cottage.

Turn left along the lane which leads to the centre of Pheasant's Hill and after a few paces, turn right onto a road marked as Bottom Hill, a typically rural, no-nonsense description. After a few paces turn left onto a signposted public footpath, at first going down some steps to then follow a narrow path between gardens before coming out at a driveway. Cross the driveway and follow another drive ahead, going downhill in the direction of a white arrow on a telegraph pole.

Just before the drive ends in front of two relatively modern houses, turn right onto a signposted public footpath which is also a crossing path. Shortly after, pass through a wooden gate and continue ahead along the right hand perimeter of a field. Your way is now along the bottom of the Hamble valley where to your left the other side of the field, is the Hamble Brook.

i **The Hamble valley.** *From this position it is easy to see why the Hamble valley was one of the first places in the Chilterns to be permanently occupied by man. The wide lush valley floor with its sparkling brook fed by springs further up the valley, provided the perfect environment for early man to settle. It was also easily accessed via the Thames, a major highway before roads became a viable option.*

The Chiltern Hills in the 20th century are an idyllic place to live, a reason for the extortionate house prices in the area. Right up until the late 19th century, the opposite was true. The tightly folded chalk hills, dense woodland and lack of accessible water reduced earning a living to a simple matter of survival. In fact, during a drought in the 19th century, it was cheaper to buy beer than water - if only that were true today! As a result of this, settlements in the Chilterns remained virtually unchanged until the turn of the century when the industrial revolution and the building of passable roads made residing in the Chilterns a relatively comfortable option There were however, a few benefits. With most of the settlements being remote and inaccessible, history which was mainly violent, often passed the Chilterns by. Unlike the rest of England, littered with lost villages wiped out by the plague, the Chilterns has relatively few, mainly abandoned for commerical reasons and not because of any major disaster.

The Hamble valley is one of a handful of river valleys in the Chilterns (the Alderbourne, Misbourne and Chess are the others), that has seen permanent occupation since the palaeolithic period, better known as the early stone age. In the neolithic period (late stone age), the valley population increased and a large settlement was established at the site of "Kimble Farm", high on the western slope.

Little changed until the coming of the Celts. The Celts brought iron, new gods and war, all of which meant a different way of life. Communities moved to the protection of hill forts and many of the river valleys were abandoned, becoming simply a place of work. The Celts however, were also efficient farmers and recognised the value of the Hamble valley, building a harbour settlement near the Thames to transpo ¿in grown in the valley.

With the Romans, the population returned to the river valleys. The harbour settlement built by the Celts was turned into a magnificent Roman villa, though its purpose remained the same. Even at this stage, the Thames was the only viable trade route to London. Excavation of the villa produced skeletons of approximately one hundred infants, a sinister discovery and still unexplained.

Little is known of what happened in the valley after the Romans left, though it is probable that many of the families returned to subsistence farming. These farmers over the years gradually organised themselves into communities and established the framework of the valley as we know it today. They also gave the valley its name, "Hamele", Saxon for "a valley with a crooked river". The word has since, of course, been corrupted to Hamble. Today, it seems peculiar that this rural retreat has over the centuries been one of the busiest and most densely populated areas of the Chilterns, its main village Hambleden, fathering and welcoming people who over the years have had a major impact on our country's history.

At the far side of the field, pass through a kissing gate and maintain your route along the right hand perimeter of the next field. The field to your right at this point is a small vineyard. At the field end, go over a stile to enter a third field and as before, carry straight on albeit this time following the left hand field perimeter. Ignore a stile on your left as you walk and continue to reach the far side of the field where you should pass through a kissing gate to continue ahead, passing to the left of some farm buildings. Pass through a second kissing gate soon after to arrive at a lane.

Turn right along the lane passing through the pretty hamlet of Colstrope. Colstrope is probably derived from the Saxon "colestre" which literally means "charcoal burners". Charcoal burning was, not surprisingly, one of the major industries in the Chilterns. Follow the lane until it bends right where you should leave it to carry straight on along a signposted public bridleway. This runs along the perimeter of "Longspring House" where you should look out for an interesting weather vane as you pass. After the house the bridleway continues between fields and if you look ahead, you can just see the windmill at the top of Turville Hill. The windmill is famous after being featured in the film "Chitty Chitty Bang Bang". *i*

i

Sometime on, the bridleway comes out at another lane beside a cottage on your left. Cross the lane and join a signposted public footpath the other side, going over a stile to do so. This goes across the centre of a field in the direction of a white arrow. At the far side of the field, you should ignore a stile on your left (providing access to a small plantation planted in 1992 to celebrate forty years reign of Her Majesty Queen Elizabeth II), and go over a stile ahead to continue across the centre of the next field as though heading for Turville Hill and its windmill. At the time of writing, this field and those surrounding it look as though they have been left fallow for several years and the mass of birdlife and wild flowers here in summer are quite stunning.

At the far end of the field, go over another stile and follow the right hand perimeter of a third field to soon pass an old manor farmhouse and farm, known appropriately as "Flint Hall". Cross a stile at the far side of the field and go over a crossing track to enter another field. This time, you should follow the left hand perimeter and at the far side, go over a stile into the next field to continue your route ahead across the centre. You should keep to the right of some hawthorn trees in front of you and approximately half way across, the village of Skirmett will suddenly come into view. At this point, you should bear gently diagonally left heading for a footpath sign to the left of a gate the other side. Go over the stile beside the gate to meet a lane.

Skirmett.

i
♟
♨

Skirmett (OS. 777899 Map 175) *is another typically beautiful Chiltern village. A jumble of flint and brick cottages lie on the valley road, facing the picturesque Elm Down, crowned by a wood and skirted by a series of fields that sweep down to the village. The name is probably derived from the Danish "scirgemot", roughly meaning "meeting place of the Shire Court". This would indicate that during the Danish occupation, Skirmett was the head village of the district and that district meetings (equivalent to today's council meetings) were held at Skirmett.*

Despite its size, the village has two hostelries. The nearest to the walk is the excellent "Old Crown", Brakspear's. This 17th century pub has been converted from three cottages which half-circle a small courtyard. Inside, you are transported back in time. A number of small rooms with

The Old Crown, Skirmett

many of their original fittings have paintings and curios from the past, carefully displayed to appear as though they have been placed casually. To the rear is the pub garden of cottage-garden style and one of the prettiest pub gardens in which I have ever had the pleasure to drink. If all this seems too good to be true, there is better to come. The Brakspear's beers which I am sure you are fed up with me enthusing over, are particularly well kept here and the food is excellent, ranging from a filling soup to main meals of such quality that it is hard to believe you are eating in a pub. The puddings are particularly good but remember, before you attempt to double your weight the hardest part of the walk is yet to come!

The second pub is further up the valley road towards Fingest. This is "The Kings Arms", a free house and a fairly large establishment. Apart from good beer and food, it also offers bed and breakfast, convenient if you over-indulge and wish to throw in your boots!

Turn left along the lane for a few paces to meet the road which runs along the length of the Hamble valley. Our way is straight on along this road, but a short detour right will bring you to "The Old Crown". As mentioned, take the road in the direction of the sign to Hambleden, Henley and Marlow and follow it as it bends left in front of a house, "Elm Down". A few paces after this, look out for a signposted public footpath on your right which you should take. This is a fenced path, easily missed, which runs between houses. After the houses, the footpath continues between fields and begins to ascend Elm Down, becoming steeper as you progress and affording excellent views left down the Hamble valley and across to "Flint Hall".

Half way up the hill, the footpath suddenly bends right and levels out, where there are lovely views over Skirmett nestling in the valley below. Your relief is short lived however, as the footpath soon bends left to continue the climb up Elm Down. Sometime on, the footpath bears right to enter Great Wood which crowns the top of the hill and follows a wide ridge where in winter when the trees are bare, you gain good views left. The path continues its gradual climb and you should continue to follow it, ignoring all minor paths off to the left or right. On almost reaching the top the footpath levels out and bends left to graduate into a track, following the edge of the hill. At this point, the wood becomes more open and the floor is covered by grass - a lovely spot to take a rest and a bite to eat if you have brought along a picnic.

The track meanders along the edge of the hill and your route is confirmed by white arrows on some of the tree trunks. Sometime later, it enters beech woodland where shortly after, the track bends right. Just after this, you should leave it to take a narrow marked footpath on the right. Take great care not to miss it. The footpath follows the line of an old fence on the right and runs parallel to the track you were on. As before, if in doubt, you should follow the white arrows painted on the tree trunks.

The footpath eventually leads out to a more prominent track which you should follow directly ahead, again in the direction of the various footpath arrows. Stay on the track as it bends right and ignore another track off to the left. Just after this, the track begins to descend and you almost feel as though you are going back on yourself. This is not the case. You have just traversed the ridge of Elm Down and are now going down the other side.

Follow the track downhill, first ignoring a track off to the right and later, another off to the left. Your route is correctly marked by the now familiar white arrows. Further down, the track bends sharp left (hairpin bend). You should leave it at this point and join a less prominent track ahead. Immediately upon joining, look out for a narrow and somewhat hidden footpath on the left, marked by a white arrow. Take this to leave the wood and then bear diagonally right across a field. Ahead of you now are the best views on the walk of Turville Down and its windmill.

On meeting a narrow path, turn left to follow it through more woodland. Pass a small gas station on your left and follow the footpath, now a wide track, ahead to reach a stile beside a gate. Cross the stile to meet a lane **(OS. 765905)**. Turn left along the lane and follow it until it bends sharp right, where you should leave it to join a signposted public bridleway on the left. Shortly after joining, the bridleway forks and you should take the right hand track, keeping to the bottom of the valley. You should now follow the bridleway for approximately one and a quarter miles until you meet a crossing path at the end of the wood **(OS. 757892)**.

(As a guide, along the way, you should ignore several minor turnings off and pass through two gates, the first being large, the second a lot smaller. After the second gate, a field will meet your route on the right and as this ends, the bridleway will meet a more prominent track onto which you should turn left to continue straight on. Essentially, if you stay on the main track, ignoring all turnings off, until you meet the crossing path at the end of the wood, then you will not go wrong). This part of the walk is delightful, passing through several changes in the surrounding woodland and lined by a variety of wild flowers in spring and summer. The wood is also home to the Muntjac deer, so keep your senses sharp.

At the end of the wood **(OS. 757892)**, turn left onto the crossing path thereby leaving the main track which leads to "Kimble Farm", the site of a neolithic settlement mentioned earlier. You will immediately meet a fork where you should take the left hand and more prominent path which continues uphill in a southerly direction through woodland. As before, you should ignore any turnings off, staying on the footpath, to eventually meet a stile which you should cross into a field. Go straight across the field, bearing very gently left, keeping the same approximate distance between you and the left hand field perimeter at all times. At the far side, cross over a stile beside a gate to reach a lane. Congratulations, you are now roughly at the highest point on the walk!

Turn left along the lane which leads through Gussetts Wood, really an extension of Great Wood, and continue for approximately a quarter of a mile until you meet a signposted public footpath on your right. Take the footpath, also marked on the trunk of a tree as footpath "44", and after a short distance, go over a crossing track (a clearing for a line of telegraph poles) to continue straight on. Your way here again is guided by white arrows painted on the trees.

Eventually, the path arrives at a stile which you should cross into a field. On a clear day you are immediately surprised by a quite unexpected and beautiful view ahead across the Thames valley into Berkshire. Turn immediately right to follow the right hand perimeter of the field and follow this round until you meet a pair of gates. Pass through the second gate into another field and continue straight ahead, thereby cutting across the right hand corner heading for a stile at the far side, easy to spot as it is marked by white topped posts. Go over the stile and turn immediately left to follow a bridleway which descends gradually between banks. This is an ancient path and could well have been the original route from the neolithic settlement at "Kimble Farm" to the Thames. After a short distance, the bridleway leaves the shelter of the banks mentioned and follows the perimeter of a field on your right. It then re-enters the protection of more banks and soon leads into another part of Great Wood.

On entering Great Wood the bridleway forks and you should take the right hand fork, the more prominent route, which descends quite steeply. Take care as in wet weather this route often doubles as a stream and the going can become very wet and slippery. There are numerous minor paths which run parallel to the bridleway here and it may be prudent in wet weather to use one of these. As you descend, the bridleway meanders through Great Wood before meeting a crossing track at the bottom of the valley, onto which you should turn right.

Almost immediately after, turn left onto another track, marked by a white arrow and ignore a track on the left here as you join. Follow the track which soon bends right and, at the same time, climbs the other side of the valley. You should ignore a track joining from the left at this point. It is not long before the track you are on virtually levels out where you can enjoy glimpses through the trees on your right across the wooded valley. Sometime later, ignore a signposted footpath on your left and carry straight on to ascend once more.

Near the top, look out for a less defined track leading off to the right and marked by white arrows. You should join this, also marked as footpath "HA 42", and follow it as it meanders along the top of the valley edge where the wood is far more open. As before, the views are quite spectacular and this may be a good place to stop for a final rest before returning to Hambleden. After a short distance, you will meet a more prominent track onto which you should turn right. Follow this for several hundred metres until you meet a crossing track onto which you should turn left, in the direction of the white arrows on the tree trunks. This soon leads out into a field where you are immediately greeted by the now familiar sight of the Hamble valley.

Follow the track ahead across the centre of the field and on meeting woodland at the far side, ignore a track off to the right to continue straight on keeping the perimeter of the wood on your right. Ahead of you now is Pheasant's Hill and you can trace th earlier parts of our walk along the far side and bottom of the valley. After approximately twenty metres, look out for a narrow footpath on the right leading through the wood, marked by a white arrow. Take this to continue your descent.

Almost at the bottom of the valley you will meet a track onto which you should turn left, still going downhill. This eventually meets a lane just after passing to the left of a white house. Cross the lane and turn right to follow it heading for Hambleden. Soon after passing the last property on your right, marked as "Woolleys" on the map, take a signposted footpath on your left which leads diagonally right across a field, still heading for Hambleden. This is a lovely way to approach the village, with the Hamble Brook running adjacent on your left and across the meadows the picturesque cottages overseeing your progress.

At the far side of the field, cross over a stile onto a lane and turn left along it to pass over the Hamble Brook. Ignore a footpath off to the left after the brook and follow the lane into the village, passing the churchyard and the equally attractive "Old Bakery". Thereafter, continue to follow the lane round to the village centre which is distinguished by an old waterpump under a horse chestnut tree. Welcome back to Hambleden.

Hambleden (OS. 785865 Map 175) *is an idyllic place at which to end the walk. This almost perfectly preserved village with its beautiful brick and flint cottages, proud church and babbling brook is probably the best example of a Chiltern village to be found. As I have already mentioned, its origins are Saxon and its name is derived from "hanelan deen" which roughly translated means "village in a crooked valley". The church which dominates the village centre dates from the 14th century and stands on the site of an earlier Saxon church. Here, like most villages, it is the church that remembers the village's past and at Hambleden what a past it is.*

The oldest item in the church is the font which probably came from the earlier Saxon church. The font was used to baptise Hambleden's earliest famous son, St. Thomas de Cantelupe. He was born at the original manor house (which stood on the site of the current manor house), in 1218 and had a reputation for fighting corruption and strongly disliked the corrupt court held by Henry III. He became a strong friend of Simon de Montfort, Earl of Leicester, the leader of the Barons opposed to the King. The friendship no doubt, was assisted by the powerful de Clare family who held the manor at the time of de Cantelupe's birth. It was Richard de Clare and his son Gilbert who were the first two signatories on the Magna Carta. They also held a castle at Bletchingley in Surrey, the history of which is detailed in "10 More Adventurous Walks in Surrey".

In 1264, de Montfort led the Barons to victory at the Battle of Lewes and de Cantelupe was appointed Chancellor of England. This post did not last long, for under a year later de Montfort was defeated and horribly killed at the Battle of Evesham. De Cantelupe feared for his life and fled to France where he had lived in earlier years. After the death of Henry III he returned to England, now a very wealthy man and set about using his wealth to build churches and houses for the poor.

In 1275, he was made Bishop of Hereford and became advisor to Edward I. Unfortunately, de Cantelupe's sometimes mis-guided morals led him into controversy with the Pope. Under threat of ex-communication de Cantelupe ex-communicated himself and set out to Rome determined to clear his name. Unfortunately, he died en route and was buried in Hereford cathedral in 1287. In the years following, a number of miracles were said to take place at his tomb which resulted in his canonisation in 1320. He was the last English man to become a saint until this century when another resident of the Chilterns, Edmund Campion, was canonised. De Cantelupe's shrine is now one of the highlights of Hereford cathedral.

In the south transept of Hambleden church stands a magnificent oaken alter. This is commonly referred to as the Wolsey Alter. It dates from the 16th century and the carving depicts the Arms of Cardinal Wolsey and Bishop Fox. The panelling was once a bed-head belonging to the Sandys family who resided at "The Vyne", now National Trust, near Basingstoke. Wolsey was a frequent visitor to "The Vyne" and it is believed he slept in the bed that went with this magnificent bed-head. It is thought the bed-head came to Hambleden with the marriage of Elizabeth Sandys to Ralph Scrope. The Scrope family held the manor during the Middle Ages and, as mentioned, it was Adrian Scrope who was one of the signatories on Charles I death warrant. There are several memorials in the church to the Scrope family, including a magnificent brass dated 1500.

In the north transept, is a superb alabaster monument to the D'Oyley family, dated 1633. Notice that some of the children are holding skulls. This was a common way of indicating that a child had died at birth or before its parents. Next to the monument is a large oak chest. This belonged to the Earl of Cardigan who like de Cantelupe, was also baptised here.

The Lady Chapel acts as a memorial to the First Viscountess Hambleden and her husband the Right Honorable W.H. Smith, M.P. They are buried just inside the entrance to the churchyard. Before becoming the Lady Chapel it was called the Sheepfold and was reserved for shepherds who would often bring their flocks to church. In the Middle Ages this was common practice and led to the use of alter rails to stop the animals defecating the alter.

Before leaving the church, make a closer inspection of the font. The broken lead mouldings are where the lid was locked to prevent pagan Saxons and witches from stealing the holy water. In the churchyard, there is a mausoleum to the Kenrick family. Doctor Kenrick was rector here in the 18th century and in 1784 built the imposing house on the eastern side of the valley overlooking the sports field. There is also a grave of yet

another famous Hambleden resident, Major George Howson, who founded the poppy factory and started the tradition of wearing poppies on Remembrance Day.

You can idle away hours wandering around Hambleden's pretty lanes. The village pump at the centre, though now little more than an ornament, was, up until 1956, the village's main water supply. There are many interesting buildings to admire and photograph but perhaps the most welcoming is "The Stag and Huntsman", a free house. This hostelry is as historic and as well preserved as the village itself. Amongst the real ales is Old Luxters Barn Ale, which is actually brewed in the village. All the food is freshly prepared and if your legs will not carry you to your car, the pub has a choice of three lovely rooms in which you can enjoy overnight accommodation. Whatever your choice, stop for at least one drink and reflect on the valley's busy past, a past that it so modestly hides.

ACCOMMODATION
The Stag and Huntsman, Hambleden. Tel: 0491 571227
On the walk, this lovely inn provides the perfect setting in which to capture the beauty of the walk through to the morning. Each room is individually furnished and downstairs, the inn provides three equally different bars in which to relax.

The Kings Arms, Skirmett. Tel: 0491 638247
Virtually on the walk, this is a large country pub popular with locals. The accommodation is ideal if you wish to do "The Christmas Cracker" and "The Great Skirmett Skirmish" on the same weekend.

Youth Hostel, Jordans YHA, Jordans. Tel: 0494 873135
Approximately fifteen miles from the walk, this is one of my favourite hostels. A wooden building set in two acres of woodland, it has a path leading down to the historic Mayflower barn and a Quaker guesthouse where you can buy a hearty breakfast.

Camping and Caravanning, Swiss Farm, Henley. Tel: 0491 573419
Approximately one and a half miles from the walk, this is a fairly large and busy site close to the Thames.

UP FLOW DOWN TOW

Distance: 10 miles (16 km)

Time: Allow approximately 4½ hours
(more if you start from Henley)

Map: Ordnance Survey Landranger Map 175

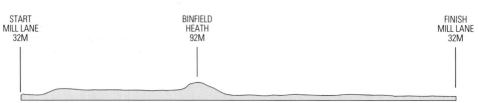

START MILL LANE 32M	BINFIELD HEATH 92M	FINISH MILL LANE 32M

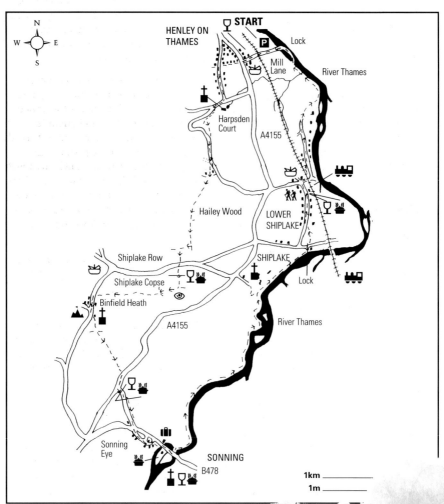

Walk Summary

Up Flow Down Tow explores the north bank of the Thames around Shiplake. It has two distinct halves, the first setting a gentle undulating course across the lower Chilterns, exploring clumps of graceful woodland and wide open fields which afford some fantastic views across the Thames valley. The second half follows the Thames tow path with all the charms one would expect from the river as well as one or two surprises. I've always said the weather can change the mood of a walk and in this case, the changes can be quite dramatic. The famous Thames valley mist can make this an eerie walk, especially near the river, and when the sun tries to break through, the effect can be quite magical. On a clear sunny day the views can be superb with the Thames sparkling as if it were made of crystal. On a cloudy day, the valley tends to act as a funnel and the atmosphere can feel quite threatening, sending you scuttling into the nearest pub! More than any other walk, I recommend you do this more than once to appreciate the different moods.

Start - OS. 771817 Map 175

The walk starts from the public car park at Mill Lane on the southern outskirts of Henley. Mill Lane leads off the A4155 on the way to Lower Shiplake. It is signposted to Mill Lane Sports Centre and starts between a Gulf petrol station and an office block, at the time of writing occupied by the company Innovex. Follow the lane over a railway line where immediately after you should turn left into the car park.

There are two good alternative starts. The first is from Mill Meadows car park at Henley (OS. 767822), which is signposted from Henley town centre. Starting here adds approximately one mile to the walk along the Thames. It also has the added benefit of finishing at Henley where you have a wide choice of establishments offering refreshments, without having to first get in your car to reach them. N.B. To join the official route from Mill Meadows car park, walk across the green to the Thames and turn right along the tow path, going up river. Continue until you reach Mill Lane where a wooden walkway extends to Marsh Lock in mid-flow. Turn right along the lane to soon meet Mill Lane car park on your right from where the walk begins. The second alternative start can be made from the railway station at Lower Shiplake, where there is a car park as well as street parking. Starting at Lower Shiplake splits the river section of the walk in half.

There are two railway stations from which you can start, Lower Shiplake which is en route and Henley on Thames where you can follow the Thames through Mill Meadows to join the route, an extension of approximately one mile.

UP FLOW DOWN TOW

To start, turn right out of the car park along Mill Lane passing over the railway line to eventually arrive at a main road, the A4155. This is beside a garage which also has a small shop in case you have forgotten your provisions for the day. N.B. A short detour along the road to your right here will bring you to "The Jolly Waterman", Brakspear's, which also offers accommodation.

Our route however, is across the road to follow a road opposite ahead, Waterman's Road. This runs between a playing field on your left and some houses on your right. After a short distance the road bends right where there is an entrance to the playing fields on your left. You should leave the road at this point, continuing ahead to now follow a signposted bridleway which runs gently uphill to soon meet another road, Harpsden Way. Cross the road and turn left along the pavement the other side, passing turnings off. The pavement later ends and you should continue ahead

33

with care, to shortly join another pavement as the road bends right in front of the imposing "Harpsden Court".

i

Harpsden Court (OS. 764808 Map 175),
*though much modernised, dates from the
13th century. It is the manor house for
Harpsden village which spreads in
small clusters further up the
valley. The name "Harpsden"
is of Saxon origin and
literally means "valley of
the harp", though the
reason for this one can
only guess at. The church
to the right of the manor
house, dates from the
12th century, but
rennovation over the
centuries has virtually
obliterated much of the*

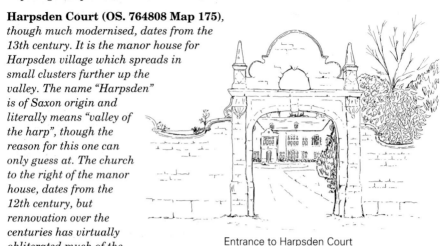

Entrance to Harpsden Court

*original structure. Opposite the church is "Harpsden Court Farm". Note the carved
wooden tiles on the ends of the barns. These were originally used for printing
patterns on wallpaper, their purpose now not dissimilar to the products they once
helped to make.*

Cross the road in front of "Harpsden Court Farm" to arrive at the church and turn
right to continue your route along the road, passing another barn on your left. A few
metres on, take a road on your left marked as Woodlands Road to almost
immediately after turn left again onto a signposted public footpath. This runs gently
uphill between banks, at first running parallel with Woodlands Road on your right.

The path slowly bends left and near the top forks (marked by white arrows). You
should take the left hand fork to follow a path which now runs in a straight line
through an area of lovely beech wood, Harpsden Wood, managed by the Woodland
Trust. Ignore any minor turnings off to soon meet Woodlands Road once more,
which has done a hairpin bend to arrive back at this point. Turn left along the road
which runs through the centre of Harpsden Wood and continue until it bends left
beside a drive on your right to "Red Hatch Lodge", fronted by brick pillars. At this
point, leave the road and follow a signposted footpath ahead. The footpath which is
fenced, at first runs between a garden on your left with the wood on your right, it
then runs between gardens before arriving at a narrow tarmac lane.

Cross the lane to enter a field the other side, opposite "Little Spinneys" and then
bear diagonally right across the centre of the field, heading for a spot roughly
twenty metres left of the far right hand corner. At the far side of the field, go over a
stile and continue ahead along a track in the direction of a yellow footpath arrow.
The track runs along the edge and then through the centre of Hailey Wood. After
passing through an avenue of laurels the track drops into a dip, where you should
ignore another track off to the left to continue up the other side and arrive at the far
side of the wood.

Continue to follow the track ahead, going over a crossing track as you do s), your
way now being between fields where to your left there are good views acros ' the

34

Thames valley to Bowsey Hill, featured in "10 Adventurous Walks in Berkshire". Later, you will meet a more prominent track on a bend and here you should turn right along the track to shortly meet a wooden bungalow on your right. At this point, you should leave the track by passing through a gap in the hedge on your left and thereafter, continue ahead along the right hand perimeter of a field. On nearing the far side of the field, the path is usually neatly mown by the residents of the house on your right, a pleasant change indeed to the mud, ruts and scrub encountered on so many of our footpaths.

Pass through an old gateway and follow a drive ahead to meet a road which you should cross to arrive at "The White Hart", Brakspear's **(OS. 756785)**. "The White Hart" is a lovely traditional pub with plenty of exposed beams and a warming open fire complete with stone surround, blackened through years of use. The pub offers a wide selection of food and on Sundays you can choose from four different roasts.

To continue, facing the pub, pass through a gap in the fence on the left hand perimeter of the car park, into a field. If you are unsure, there is a footpath sign beside the road indicating the direction. Once in the field, turn right and then bear diagonally left across the centre, heading for the far corner identifiable by a pair of electricity poles. On reaching the far corner, turn right in the direction of a footpath sign, now walking beneath the electricity wires. There are fine views to your left here across the Thames valley into Berkshire and on a clear day, ahead of you are the twin gas storage tanks which mark the centre of Reading.

On meeting the next electricity pole, turn diagonally right in the direction of another footpath sign across the centre of a field. At the far side, pass through a gap in the hedge and go over a crossing track to enter a field on your left the other side (do not go into the field on your right). Continue ahead along the right hand perimeter of the field and when the perimeter makes a small loop to the right, leave it to carry straight on missing the loop out. You will shortly rejoin the perimeter and should follow it to the far side of the field, where the path enters Shiplake Copse.

Follow a prominent path ahead, uphill through the copse, the floor of which is a dense carpet of bluebells in spring.

Bluebells *in late spring are an attractive feature on any Chiltern walk. They are one of the few flowers which can survive under the thick beechwood canopy. The reason for their success is that they bloom before the trees get their leaves and block out the light. They are virtually the only flower that does this, the reason why they have such a monopoly on the woodland floor. Bluebells struggle to survive close to other plants and because of this are only usually found in woodland environments.*

The old term for bluebells is "crowtoes". Their bulbs contain starch and were used by the Elizabethans to stiffen their elaborate ruffs. Over the years, their bulbs have also been crushed to make glue.

Either side of the path, streams wind snake-like into the fields below. These rise from springs at Shiplake Row and on leaving the copse, flow underground into the Thames. On nearing the far side of the copse, the path twists to enter a field on your right. Here you should maintain your route by following the left hand perimeter of the field, with Shiplake Copse on your left. Keeping to the left hand perimeter, you will soon leave the copse behind and at the far side of the field, should pass through an old iron kissing gate to continue ahead along the left hand perimeter of the next field.

At the far side of the field, you will arrive at a road onto which you should turn left to enter the village of Binfield Heath.

Binfield Heath (OS. 743780 Map 175) *like many of the villages along this stretch of the Chilterns bordering the Thames, was created from the need for safe grazing land when the Thames valley flooded. Many of these temporary settlements kept the name of their sister villages on the Thames and Sonning Common and Shiplake Bottom are two examples. As these higher settlements became villages in their own right, recriprocal agreements were signed allowing the Thames-side villages access to grazing land in return for access rights to the river. These agreements were later taken into consideration when developing parish boundaries and consequently, the parishes here are long and narrow, running from the hills down to the Thames.*

As a result of Binfield Heath's origin as a temporary settlement for riverside dwellers, the village is spread out with no real centre. It does have a couple of pubs but visiting these would mean a considerable detour and unless you are suffering from withdrawal symptons, are not really worth it. The only village church is passed en route, an unusual gothic style building built in 1835.

Follow the road through the village to soon pass the church where you should ignore a road opposite the church, Gravel Road. Shortly after passing the church, take a track left which at first passes to the right of "Radbrook House", before continuing between fields. You will eventually arrive at a crossing track which you should ignore to follow a fenced track ahead, again between fields. This soon begins to descend and later passes between Roundwood Wood on your right and The Firs on the left. The name The Firs can be confusing as the wood has every tree but firs!

The track soon leaves the woodland behind to once again continue between fields. After a short level stretch it makes one final descent to meet the A4155 once more. Cross the road and turn right to follow it, keeping to the narrow grass verge for safety. Ahead of you now are the twin gas

Binfield Church

storage tanks at Reading with the town centre also visible. You will soon arrive at "The Flowing Spring", a Fullers pub named after a spring which rises nearby. It is the only pub with this name in Britain. The entrance is reached by climbing a series of iron steps from the car park and once through the door, you will find yourself in a lively horseshoe bar. A number of humorous pictures adorn the walls, a reflection of the landlord who is ready with a witty remark for any situation. The food is basic but well cooked - traditional pub grub. If you are lucky, you can enjoy your meal whilst being accompanied by music from the pub piano.

At "The Flowing Spring", from the A4155, turn left into Spring Lane, signposted to Sonning and follow it to soon cross the pretty Berry Brook. Thereafter, keep to the lane for approximately twenty metres, where you should leave it to join a signposted public footpath on your left, going over a stile to do so.

After the stile, turn immediately right and follow the right hand perimeter of a field, thereby walking parallel with the lane. At the end of the field, go over a wooden plank bridge and then a stile into another field, where you should continue ahead along the right hand perimeter. At the end of this field, go over a stile to rejoin the lane, turning left to follow it. This soon brings you to the B478 which you should cross to join a tarmac path the other side. Pass through a wooden gate and continue ahead, along what was the original course of the B478, passing a lovely old rambling house on your right.

After passing the entrance to Reading Sailing Club on your right, the road bends left and here you should leave it to follow a lane ahead which leads into the village of Sonning Eye. Follow the lane through the village, later bending sharp left opposite the beautiful "Long Gardens". Shortly after, turn right onto a tarmac path which starts beside the village notice board. The path passes between some farm buildings before coming out at the river Thames beside the "The French Horn Hotel".

Sonning Eye (OS. 752759 Map 175) *until the late 19th century, although in Oxfordshire, came under the administration of Sonning parish in Berkshire on the opposite bank of the river. This was unique for a Thames-side village, for with the river acting as a county boundary, if the settlement spread across both banks they would be administered separately and have their own identities as with Goring and Streatley further up river.*

The name Sonning is of Saxon origin and loosely translated means "followers of a man called Sunna", who was probably a Saxon Chieftain. Eye is derived from the Saxon "Eg" which describes a place or settlement on an island. Many islands on the Thames have similar names, for example, "Ait" or "Eyot". These stem from a similar Saxon word, "Egath" which means "small island". The frequency of these names give some idea of how well the Thames was used during the Saxon era. The name Sonning Eye, considering the above, has led to speculation that where we are now standing was once an island. Before much of the Thames was drained forming its current route, the river was much wider and shallower. Centuries ago, it is quite likely that the river stretched to where "The Flowing Spring" pub is today. The name "Thames" is much older than "Sonning" or "Eye". It is derived from the Celtic word, "Tamesis" which means "dark or large river". There are several rivers in England with names derived from the same word, two examples are the Tamar which separates Cornwall from Devon and more locally, the river Thame.

Sonning, on the far bank in Berkshire, is worth a short detour, if only to visit the excellent "Bull Inn", Wethereds. The pub is opposite the village church and can be reached via the churchyard. Up until the reign of Elizabeth I, there was a palace beside the church which belonged to the Bishops of Salisbury. In 1399, Henry IV, son of John O Gaunt of Hungerford (see "10 Adventurous Walks in Berkshire"), imprisoned the child Queen of Richard II after Henry had forced her husband to abdicate. Richard was imprisoned at Pontefract Castle and died a year later, probably murdered. The poor innocent Queen remained a prisoner, ignorant of her husband's death. Apart from a mound and some brickwork in the churchyard wall, there is little evidence of the former palace.

As well as "The Bull Inn", there are a number of tea rooms and restaurants hidden amongst Sonning's pretty streets.

Turn left to meet the B478 once more and then right to follow it over an arm of the Thames (Sonning Backwater), where the road takes you onto an island with an old mill, now converted into a theatre and restaurant. If you are staying locally, this makes for an interesting evening out.

i If you wish to visit Sonning, continue ahead over a narrow brick bridge controlled by traffic lights (you will have to retrace your steps to rejoin our route). *The bridge which is reputed to be the oldest on the Thames, was built in 1772. Before this, there was a wooden bridge built and maintained by the Bishops of Salisbury. Recently, the bridge was temporarily closed and the residents of Sonning demonstrated their frustration at the volume of motor traffic using the bridge by adding a sign, "Close it Permanently".*

To continue our route, cross the road opposite the theatre entrance and at the other side, go over an arch bridge which takes you back over the Sonning Backwater. After the bridge, pass through a small gate on your right to join the Thames tow path. Our route from here is along the river to return to the start. Do not make the mistake however, of relaxing too soon as you are still only half way!

As you follow the tow path, the buildings of Sonning on the far bank soon disappear and you will find yourself following the Thames through a landscape of flat misty fields and gentle rolling hills. This scenery does not change for several miles, but somehow one never tires of walking beside a river, especially with the ever passing river traffic which can either be interesting or amusing, depending upon the skill of the crew! After approximately one and a quarter miles, the fields around you are suddenly broken by a number of attractive houses on the far bank, designed to afford their owners the best possible view over the river. They stand where St. Patrick's Stream enters the Thames. The stream is an arm of the river Loddon, the waters of which rise in Hampshire and travel through Berkshire to reach this point.

The houses very quickly end and once again, you are alone with the Thames. Not long after, at the end of a field, the path passes through a wooden gate to continue through an area of scrub, at the same time passing an island in mid-river, Hallsmead Ait. The island in spring is alive with the sounds of birds raising their young. The path eventually leaves the scrub via a second wooden gate and your route continues once more through a field. At this point, the river bends right around a second island, The Lynch, where at the same time you will just discern the rooftops of Shiplake village and its famous college ahead of you, above the trees.

At the far side of the field, follow the tow path across a bridge over an inlet with an attractive boathouse belonging to Shiplake College. After the bridge you will arrive at a small neatly cut grass clearing where the boys from Shiplake College launch their boats. Before continuing, it is worth making a short detour at this point to visit Shiplake church. To do this, take a track left (not the tarmac drive) between boathouses and follow it until you arrive at a junction just before an entrance to a field ahead. Here, take a path right going uphill to soon arrive at the church.

i **Shiplake Church (OS. 767783 Map 175)** *commands a lofty position above the*
✝ *Thames. Guide books written at the turn of the century enthuse about the views over*
■ *the Thames from the church porch. Today, this is obscured by trees, though if you walk through the churchyard to the right of the church, you can appreciate a similar*

view. The church itself dates from the 12th century, though it was much altered by the Victorians. The most notable feature are the church's medieval glass windows. The glass came from the abbey of St. Bertin at St. Omer in France. During the French Revolution, the monks removed the glass and buried it for safe keeping. It was later sold to the Vicar of Henley who presented it to Shiplake.

On 13th June, 1850 the church witnessed the wedding of the poet, Alfred Lord Tennyson, to Emily Sellwood, a cousin of the Vicar's wife. Emily came from the village of Aldworth, near Goring, further up the Thames. Her parents are buried at the village church. It is said that instead of paying a wedding fee, Tennyson presented the Vicar with a poem. A copy of the poem can be purchased at the church.

Returning to our route, walk across the grass area and continue along the tow path which at this point runs between a copse and the river. A short time on, another bridge takes you over a second inlet and thereafter, past the magnificent "Shiplake House" on your left. The small island that divides the Thames at this point is called Phillimore's Island, after Sir Robert Phillimore, a much revered 19th century judge. Continue to meet and cross a stile and keep to the tow path, walking through fields, now approaching Shiplake Lock. On drawing level with the lock, go over a stile in front of a brick and flint wall and turn left to shortly meet a road. First however, I recommend a short detour right to visit Shiplake Lock.

At the road, turn right and after a few paces, opposite "Mill House", turn left over a stile to follow a fenced path between fields. (The "Mill House" incidentally, was once home to another Phillimore, a Colonel Robert Phillimore, who worked with General Eisenhower on "Operation Overlord"). Go over another stile soon after and continue ahead along the left hand perimeter of the next field and at the far side, go over a stile on your left into another field. Bear diagonally right across the corner of the field to meet a drive the other side.

Turn left along the drive and go over Lash Brook to soon meet a lane. Turn right along the lane passing the first houses of Lower Shiplake and keep to the lane looking out for the attractive weatherboarded Lash Brook chapel along the way. Ignore all turnings off and continue to eventually arrive at a crossroads beside "The Baskerville Arms", Whitbread, your last chance for a drink before we finish. There is also a small general stores here, "The Corner Shop", which sells just about everything you could need. Turn right at the crossroads along Station Road and cross the railway line to then turn immediately left onto an unmarked path. This runs between the railway line on your left and houses on the right.

After a short distance you will meet a crossing path onto which you should turn right, to immediately pass through a kissing gate before following another fenced path. Go over a gravel drive just after which you should turn left along a residential road, passing between a number of magnificent properties. Ignore all turnings off and keep to the road which later bends right after the entrance to "Bolney Court" and eventually ends in front of a private drive. Here, take a fenced path on the left which runs parallel with the drive. To your right now is a magnificent garden complete with its own minature railway and purpose-built station together with a working clock-tower, handy if you have forgotten your watch.

The drive on your right soon bends right to service a house, "Fair Acres", where you should keep to the path as it continues ahead between fields. After a short distance, go over a stile and then a wooden plank bridge into a field, where you should carry straight on to shortly meet and follow the river Thames downriver. Your way is now, once again, along the old tow path, passing a couple of charming properties on the opposite bank, one of which is the boathouse for "Park Place", once home to the father of George III. Eventually, the field ends and you should pass through a wooden gate to follow a fenced path ahead. This takes you onto a wooden walkway which in turn leads you out into the centre of the river Thames to Marsh Lock. This is a magical spot and a fitting end to the walk, with the Thames displaying a beauty hardly matched anywhere else on the river.

A smart boat house

Pass the lock itself and continue ahead along another walkway which takes you past the front of the weir, where the gentle Thames is momentarily transformed into a seething torrent. Follow the walkway to arrive back on dry land at Mill Lane where you should, albeit reluctantly, leave the river to follow the lane ahead. (If you started from Mill Meadows at Henley, you should turn right along the tow path and retrace your steps to the car park). Keep to the lane passing a number of attractive houses to soon arrive back at the car park, our starting point.

ACCOMMODATION

The French Horn, Sonning Eye. Tel: 0734 692204
On the walk, this is the place to stay if you wish to spoil yourself. An hotel for over one hundred and fifty years, it has a beautiful location overlooking the river Thames. The interior can only be described as tasteful and luxurious. Most of the rooms overlook the river and in addition, there are four luxury riverside cottages.

Holmwood, Binfield Heath. Tel: 0734 478747
Just over half a mile from the walk, accommodation is in a large country Georgian house set in thirty acres of ground. All the rooms are en suite and if you feel you need further exercise, a hard tennis court is available.

Youth Hostel, Streatley YHA, Streatley. Tel: 0491 872278
Approximately ten miles from the walk, the recently refurbished Streatley hostel now offers small family rooms as well as the normal dorms we all know. The hostel itself is a large Victorian house only a few paces from "The Bull Inn".

Camping and Caravanning, Swiss Farm, Henley. Tel: 0491 573419
Approximately two miles from the walk, this is a fairly large and busy site close to the Thames.

THE HELL FIRE HIKE

Distance: 10½ miles (17 km)

Time: Allow approximately 5½ hours

Map: Ordnance Survey Landranger Maps 165/175

| START
BRADENHAM
103M | CRYERS
HILL
170M | DOWNLEY
188M | FINISH
BRADENHAM
103M |

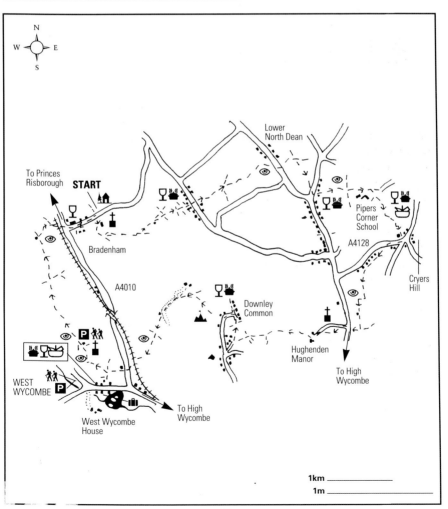

Walk Summary

This is a walk packed with interest and complimented by wonderful scenery and stunning views. The walk passes no less than three large country houses, two of which are in the hands of the National Trust. In addition, you can visit the infamous Hell Fire Caves, the setting for the meetings of the Hell Fire Club in the 18th century and from which this adventure takes its name. Apart from houses and caves, it is possible to sample no less than seven pubs en route. With this in mind, perhaps I should have named this adventure "Paradise Found"!

Start - OS. 828921 Map 165

The walk starts from St. Botolph church at Bradenham. The church is opposite the Bradenham Youth Hostel which is housed in the old village school. Street parking is possible in the village where there is a small parking area beside the Youth Hostel. There is also a small car park beside the village cricket pavilion, reached by taking a track which leads from the road near "The Red Lion" and skirts the green to reach the pavilion itself.

Bradenham is just off the A4010 in between Princes Risborough and West Wycombe. The village is signposted and the turning is easily identified as it is beside "The Red Lion" pub. The nearest motorway is the M40 with the nearest exit being exit 4, signposted to Wycombe and Marlow. From there, simply stay on the A4010 following the signs to Aylesbury until you reach Bradenham.

An alternative start can be made from West Wycombe where there are several car parks. The nearest railway station is at Saunderton, approximately one mile from the walk. At weekends, trains stop at Saunderton roughly every three hours.

THE HELL FIRE HIKE

The walk starts from another of those almost perfectly preserved Chiltern villages, though Bradenham is perhaps more famous for once having been the home of Isaac D'Israeli, the father of Benjamin D'Israeli who was to become one of our most revered Prime Ministers.

Bradenham (OS. 828971 Map 165) nestles in an idyllic location at the bottom of a wide sweeping valley, protected on either side by majestic Chiltern beech wood. The village encircles a large sloping green dominated at the higher end by the 16th century manor house and the village church. It was to the manor that Isaac D'Israeli brought

Bradenham Manor

42

his son, Benjamin, to live. The year was 1829 and Benjamin was just thirteen. After having been brought up in the London "smoke", Bradenham must have been a wondrous place for the boy and throughout his life he always returned to the Chilterns to relax, even buying his own manor at Hughendon, though this is another story.

Isaac D'Israeli, the son of an Italien jew, was born in London in 1766. Although an active member of the jewish community, he gradually drifted away from his faith and had his children, including Benjamin, baptised in the Christian church. He became famous in his own right as a writer studying people in history, in particular his literary illustration of Charles I, and his study of authors, "Curiosities of Literature" and "Calamities of Authors", brought him world acclaim. He lived at Bradenham until his death in 1848, up to which time he was to see his son become a Member of Parliament. He did not survive long enoung, however, to see Benjamin become Prime Minister. Isaac was buried at the village church, literally just the other side of his garden wall. Surprisingly, a modest marble tablet is his only memorial.

The church, dedicated to St. Botolph, was originally Saxon though little of this era can be identified today. Your entrance is by the oldest doorway in the county, dating from around 1100. One can only begin to imagine the scenes it has witnessed over the centuries. The 15th century tower houses two of the oldest bells in the country.

St. Botolph, is a somewhat mysterious character with none of his life save a few lines, being recorded in the Anglo-Saxon Chronicle. One of the first Saxon saints, he is known to have been educated in France and returned to England as a missionary at Norfolk, ruled by King Anna. In the year 654, Anna was killed by the resentful pagans and the Anglo-Saxon Chronicle states that in the same year, Botolph started his monastery at Icanhoh. Where Icanhoh was remains a mystery to this day, as two centuries later marauding Danes destroyed the monastery and all traces have now disappeared. In the 10th century, Botolph's body was exhumed and divided into three to receive honourable burials around the country. A century later, King Edward the Confessor demanded that St. Botolph deserved a resting place in his new abbey at Westminster and the body was divided one more time. The Saint, who was canonised for his efforts in establishing one of the first monasteries in pagan Briton, now lies at rest at four holy sites around the country.

There are a number of other interesting buildings encircling the green, nearly all protected by the National Trust. At the lower end, the village meets the A4010 where you will find the village pub, "The Red Lion", a free house. Tempting though it might be, remember that there are no less than seven pubs on this walk and if you want to finish, I suggest you make "The Red Lion" the seventh and not the first!

To start, from the parking area opposite the church and beside the youth hostel, cross the road and continue ahead along the edge of the green, passing in front of the church and then the majestic "Bradenham Manor", now a management college. Here you are immediately presented with lovely views right across the cricket green to Averingdown which we will traverse during the last stages of our walk.

On reaching the far side of the green you will arrive at a parking area beside a cricket pavilion. Continue ahead and on meeting a track turn left to follow the perimeter wall of "Bradenham Manor". The track leads uphill and soon forks where, at the same point, there is a footpath leading off to the right. You should ignore the footpath and take the left hand fork, thereby continuing to follow the wall of "Brad___ ___ Manor". A few metres on, the track forks once more and this time you should take the right hand fork, in the direction of a blue bridleway arrow, now bearing away from the perimeter wall of the manor.

Ignore another track off to the right immediately after, thereby continuing ahead to shortly meet another track (the original track) onto which you should turn left. This continues uphill and soon breaks clear of the trees, arriving at a grass clearing with neatly manicured hedges. Carry straight on here to shortly pass a typical brick and flint Chiltern cottage on your right. Soon after, the track bends sharp right heading for "Bradenham Hill Farmhouse" and here you should leave it to continue ahead along a marked bridleway (blue arrow). Do not make the mistake of taking either of the two turnings off to the left.

After a short distance, the bridleway forks in front of a wooden post with several blue arrows. Take the left hand fork to commence your traverse through the beautiful open woodland of Naphill Common. Ensure you keep to the main path at all times ignoring any turnings off, to soon meet and follow a line of telegraph poles. You will shortly arrive at a large junction of paths where you should continue ahead, in the direction of the blue arrows, thereby leaving the line of telegraph poles which bear left at this point. Almost immediately after, another path leads off to the left which you should ignore and carry straight on to shortly pass a small pond on the right, surrounded by beautiful beech woodland.

Ignore another path off to the left at the pond to carry straight on along a now much narrower path. If you do not immediately pass the pond, you have taken the wrong path and should retrace your steps to find the correct route. As before, you should ignore any turnings off, thereby keeping to the main path. Sometime later the path forks and you should take the right hand fork, which at the time of writing is unmarked. The path runs in a straight line through woodland and again you should ignore any turnings off to the left or right, to eventually reach a prominent crossing path marked by a wooden post. Go over the crossing path and continue along a narrow path, in the direction of a yellow public footpath arrow.

After a few paces you will arrive at a rough track in front of some houses, the start of Naphill village. A short detour left along the track for approximately fifty metres will bring you to "The Black Lion", Courage, a good traditional pub which is open all day. You will have to retrace your steps to continue the walk. Returning to our route, cross the track to join a path ahead marked by a "Prohibited Cycling" sign, ignoring a turning off to your right almost immediately after joining. The path runs between houses to soon meet a road in front of "Moseley Lodge" **(OS. 843974 Map 165)**.

Cross the road and join a signposted footpath the other side, going over a stile into a field to do so. Go straight across the field heading for the far right hand corner, passing the lovely "Great Moseley Farm" on your right as you walk. At the far corner, go over a stile beside a gate and continue ahead along a track across a larger field. At the far side, pass through a gap in the hedge and continue ahead along the left hand perimeter of the next field. Do not make the mistake of taking the path on your left which runs across the centre of the field on your left. Your route will shortly begin to descend, heading for Seer Wood.

Just prior to reaching the field corner take a narrow path on your left to enter the wood, thereby continuing your route downhill. You should ignore any turnings off to the left or right upon joining and continue downhill through a shallow valley. If you are lucky enough to be walking this way in late spring, then the bluebells here are a delight. On meeting a fence (as a guide in case the fence later disappears, this is approximately fifty metres into the wood and is marked by arrows on a tree), bear left to follow the path up the side of the valley and thereafter, along the valley side.

Sometime later, after passing along the edge of a small clearing, the path leaves the wood (after going over a stile), to arrive at open grass hillside with superb views of rolling Chiltern countryside. Immediately below you is the picturesque hamlet of Lower North Dean. "Dean" is a very common old English name meaning "in the valley". From here, go diagonally right downhill heading for a stile at the right hand field perimeter and after crossing the stile into the next field, maintain your route by cutting across the left hand corner, making for another stile visible ahead. Go over the stile and cross a road at the bottom of the valley to join a signposted footpath the other side, passing through a pair of metal gates into a field.

Continue ahead along the left hand perimeter of the field to ascend the other side of the valley, where as you near the top you should look out for a stile on your left. Do not go over the stile but take a path immediately on your right (not second right), to cross the centre of the field heading for the houses in Hughenden valley below. At the far side of the field, pass through a kissing gate to meet a road in front of "The Harrow" pub, Courage, **(OS. 861976 Map 165)**. "The Harrow", the second pub on the walk, is another excellent traditional Chiltern pub offering a good range of home cooked food.

Cross the road passing in front of the pub and walk through the pub car park and go over a stile to thereafter, follow a path gently uphill between gardens. This soon leads to a small cul-de-sac which you should cross to join a path the other side, leading uphill with the help of some steps. As you progress you are afforded lovely views left up the Dean valley and the earlier part of our route. Approximately half way up the steps disappear (the builder probably died of exhaustion!) and the rest of the way is left for you to negotiate as best you can.

After what can seem an age, particularly if you stopped for some ale at "The Harrow", the path levels out to follow the line of a field on your left, with views to your left over the northern extension of the Hughenden valley. Continue ahead to later go over a crossing path, after which the path follows the perimeter of Pipers Corner School. Go over a stile and carry straight on across a field and approximately two thirds of the way across, go over a stile on your right (take care not to miss this), to cross the school drive and join an unmarked path the other side which runs along the right hand edge of an open garden.

Go over another stile and cross a small lane, passing through a kissing gate the other side and continue ahead along the left hand perimeter of a field on your right. Do not make the mistake of going into the field on your left. The route descends gently and at the far side of the field you should go over a stile and follow a prominent path ahead along the edge of Gomms Wood. Your meeting with the wood is a short one, as it is not long before your route follows the left hand perimeter of another field.

At the far side of the field follow the path ahead along the perimeter of another school, Great Kingshill School, to shortly come out at a main road, the A4128, at Cryers Hill **(OS. 874969 Map 165)**. A short detour left here (thirty metres) will take you to the third pub on our route, "The White Lion", Courage, and the village Post Office. Our route however, is across the A4128, where you should turn right at the other side to follow it for approximately forty metres, before turning left onto a signposted public footpath.

The footpath crosses a small enclosure and then passes through two kissing gates to enter a field. Carry straight on across the field following the left hand perimeter and at the far side, go through another kissing gate to thereafter follow the left hand perimeter of the next field. Your way here is along the left hand side of a valley with open views to your right across the Hughenden valley. At the field end, pass through yet another kissing gate into a third field and maintain your route passing through a kissing gate at the far side, to follow a path through a long copse, also part of a series of gardens. After the copse the path becomes hedged and runs between fields and where gaps in the hedge allow, you are afforded more lovely views to your right over the Hughenden valley.

The path eventually meets a stile which you should cross into a field. Turn right and follow the field perimeter round, passing to the left of a large barn along the way, after which you will gain fine views right to Hughenden church, our next destination. At the far side of the field go over a stile and turn right onto a fenced path which leads downhill, heading for Hughenden church. You will shortly meet the main road, the A4128, for the second time and as before, you should cross it.

Turn left the other side and after approximately twenty metres, turn right onto the driveway of "Hughenden Manor", National Trust. Pass the gatehouse, "Church Lodge", and follow the drive as it crosses a small brook, after which you should pass through a gate and continue to follow the drive ahead. Soon after, fork left to enter Hughenden churchyard, the church being dedicated to St. Michael and All Angels.

St. Michael and All Angels, Hughenden (OS. 864955 Map 165) *is famous for being the church of "Hughenden Manor" and the resting place of Benjamin D'Israeli. It must also rank as one of England's prettiest churches in one of the most delightful settings in the Chilterns. The church as we see it today, is mainly Victorian, giving the impression that it was built for the house. In fact, this is untrue as there has been a church here since Saxon times, which for centuries served a small scattered village.*

The village slowly moved north up the valley and it was probably only the large manor house which ensured the church's survival. Hughenden is derived from "Hitchenden". "Hitchin" is a Celtic word meaning "dry river" and "den" is probably derived from "dean" which, as we have already learned, is old English for "in the valley". This would indicate that the stream which flows through the valley often dried up.

Inside the church, as you would expect, are a number of worthy memorials. The most famous is a memorial in the chancel to Benjamin D'Israeli. This is unique as it was donated by Queen Victoria and is the only example of a memorial erected to a subject by a reigning monarch. Beside the memorial hangs a banner and the insignia of the Order of the Garter. These were taken from St. George's Chapel, Windsor, again at the wish of Queen Victoria.

In the north chancel once known as the de Montfort Chapel, are several stone figures of knights. These are in fact, 16th century forgeries errected by the vain Wellesbourne family to try and convince people that they were descendants of Simon de Montfort. To some extent their efforts succeeded as for many years the stone figure of a knight in armour of chainmail with crossed legs, was thought to be a son of Simon de Montfort. We now know however, know that their claims were false.

Outside the church is the D'Israeli family vault and the tomb of Benjamin D'Israeli. Buried with Benjamin are close members of his family as well as a fervent admirer,

Mrs. Sarah Brydges-Willyams. Mrs. Brydges-Willyams begged D'Israeli that she might share his grave and offered him a small fortune for the privilege. As you can see from the inscription on the tomb, she achieved her greatest wish.

Follow the tarmac path uphill through the churchyard and exit beside the beautiful "Church House". The house was originally built to house a small religious commune consisting of six monks and a Prior. After leaving the churchyard, carry straight on still going uphill, to soon reach and pass through a gate onto a drive, though before going any further I suggest you take a breather and enjoy the views back to the church and the Hughenden valley. To continue, bear left along the drive in the direction of a sign for "Deliveries and Disabled Visitors" and pass the entrance to "The Old Vicarage". You will soon arrive at the entrance of "Hughenden Manor".

Hughenden Manor, National Trust (OS. 861955 Map 165), *was constructed in the 18th century and replaced an earlier farmhouse. In 1848, Benjamin D'Israeli remembering his roots, after much difficulty, purchased the house. To complete the purchase he borrowed heavily from friends, including £25,000 from Lord George Bentinck. A crisis occurred in 1857 when Lord Bentinck called in his loan. D'Israeli scraped by for several years after this but was saved from having to leave the property by Mrs. Brydges-Willyams who left him £30,000 in her will. D'Israeli as we know, in return granted her her wish to be buried beside him and was probably very happy to do so, for he clearly loved "Hughenden Manor" and was loathe to leave it.*

The money from Mrs. Brydges-Willyams also allowed D'Israeli to complete the gothic alterations started by the house's previous owner. Together with his wife, they made many improvements to the grounds and after her death, D'Israeli concentrated his efforts on modernising the church. The house apart from being his home, a place to escape from the rigours of Parliament, was also in contrast, an extension of his office at Westminster.

D'Israeli lived and breathed politics having strong principles which more than once led to his resignation. He would entertain both friends and rivals at the house, including Queen Victoria, with whom he struck up a particularly close relationship. In between politics, he also managed to continue with his other love, writing. In fact, it was through his first novel, "Vivien Grey", that he first rose to fame. As Prime Minister, D'Israeli steered Britain through what many consider to be the country's most glorious period. Though strong and determined he was also a good tactician and diplomat and gained the respect of many foreign leaders. He finally retired in 1880 after losing heavily at the General Election and returned to Hughenden to concentrate on his writing. He died in London the following year and was buried at Hughenden in his beloved Chilterns.

The house today is much as Benjamin D'Israeli would remember it, especially the study in which he worked. To visit the house is to visit a part of England's history and a fascinating experience.

Unless you intend visiting the manor, continue along the drive and as it bends left into the staff car park leave it to join a public bridleway ahead. This immediately descends through Hanging Wood where shortly after joining, you should ignore a prominent crossing path and continue ahead, still going downhill. At the bottom of the hill the bridleway leaves the wood and continues between fields. To your left here is "Manor Farm".

As you continue, the bridleway gradually bends left to enter Common Wood. Ignore a marked footpath (yellow arrow) on your left as you enter the wood and carry straight on. The bridleway leads gently uphill through Common Wood and eventually arrives at a junction of paths beside a National Trust sign for the Hughenden Estate. Continue ahead, ignoring all turnings off to the left and right (take great care not to make the mistake of turning left after the National Trust sign), keeping to the bridleway which runs gently uphill, to soon after pass to the left of the lovely but simple "Well Cottage" (1813).

A few paces on you will meet a crossing path just in front of the first houses of the hamlet of Downley. Turn right onto the crossing path to immediately go up a small rise to meet a track onto which you should turn right. This in turn almost immediately ends and your way is directly ahead, passing between two wooden posts, to cross Downley Common. In 1871 a local man witnessed what he believed to be a U.F.O. above the common. His sighting caused quite a stir at the time, though many believed that it was nothing more than an overactive imagination.

Follow a grass path across the common, do not fork left, and at the far side join a track which runs alongside some houses on your right. This leads to a lane on your left which you should take. First though, I recommend you continue ahead for a few paces more to arrive at the excellent "Le de Spencers Arms", Fullers, a beautiful traditional pub complete with sloping garden which is full of snowdrops in spring and lit in summer with coloured lights. You will have to retrace your steps to rejoin our route.

Returning to our route, take the lane left to skirt the cricket green and just before reaching a bus stop, take a signposted public footpath on your right. As a guide, this is also beside a small clubhouse. The footpath initially follows the drive of a house where, after a few paces, you should leave it to pass through a kissing gate on your left. Thereafter, turn right to follow the edge of a small field.

At the far side of the field, pass through another kissing gate and continue ahead along the right hand perimeter of the next field. You now have lovely views left of the Chiltern hills around West Wycombe and you can just see the top of the mausoleum and church, identified by its golden ball, at West Wycombe itself, our next destination.

At the far side of the field continue ahead along a prominent path which descends the side of a wooded valley and at the bottom, turn left onto a crossing path to follow the valley downhill. The path leads down to a tarmac drive onto which you should turn left. Follow the drive until it bends left beside a parking area and small brick and weatherboarded farm building and here leave it, crossing the parking area, at the far side going over a stile to carry straight on, downhill, along a grass path which divides two fields. The mausoleum and church at West Wycombe ahead to your right, are now a major feature of the landscape.

At the end of the fields go over a stile, cross a track and continue up a bank the other side to meet and cross a second stile into a field. Cross the field following the right hand perimeter to go over the crest of a low hill, where you gain yet more good views to the mausoleum and church, now on your right. Below the hill is the beautiful "Flinthall Farm" and just before it, the railway line from Princes Risborough. Also, in winter when the trees are bare you can just discern "West Wycombe House", a fine paladin mansion, directly ahead.

At the far side of the field the path passes through a gap in a hedge and enters another field where you should continue ahead, descending along the right hand perimeter and heading for a railway arch. At the far side of the field go over a stile, pass under the railway and at the other side, pass through a gate and bear diagonally left across the centre of a field, heading for a footpath sign the other side. This is just left of "Flinthall Farm". At the end of the field you will meet a main road, the A4010, which you should cross with care to go over a "V" stile the other side into another field.

Continue ahead along the right hand perimeter of the field and pass to the left of "Flinthall Farm" and approximately half way across the field and at the end of a line of beech trees, cross a stile on your right into another field. Turn immediately left and follow the left hand perimeter of this field uphill, now heading for the mausoleum. On reaching the end of the field pass through a kissing gate onto a narrow lane. From here you have a choice. If you wish to visit West Wycombe and the Hell Fire Caves as well as the fourth, fifth and sixth pubs on our walk, then turn left along the lane taking either the left or right hand fork, both of which lead down into the village.

West Wycombe (OS. 828948 Map 175) *has been made famous by the Dashwood family who still live at the fine paladin manor house, now in the care of the National Trust. In fact, the entire village (consisting of many fine half timbered buildings), including a pub, is protected by the National Trust. The village is surrounded by monuments built by Sir Francis Dashwood, 15th Baron Le Dispencer and Chancellor of the Exchequer, 1761 to 1762.*

It was Sir Francis who built the mausoleum and re-styled St. Lawrence church with its distinctive golden ball, on the hill above the village. Both are visited later on the walk. It was also Sir Francis who re-modelled a previously Queen Anne house into the fine paladin mansion and had Capability Brown landscape the grounds which now include one of the best collections of follies in England. Sir Francis also tunnelled the infamous Hell Fire Caves. The caves, which can be visited for a small fee, were excavated around 1750 to provide material for the London to Oxford road which had become notorious for its deep ruts. It would have been easier to simply extend the small quarry from where the caves started but Sir Francis obviously had an ulterior motive for tunnelling. The tunnel when finished stretched a quarter of a mile into the hill and at its deepest was three hundred feet below ground. Its peculiar winding shape and numerous small caves had a symbolic meaning to Sir Francis and, it has been suggested, is taken from the Eleusinian mysteries of ancient Greece.

In 1766 Sir Francis transferred the meeting place of his infamous Monks of Medmenham (see "Defeating the Danes") to the caves at West Wycombe. Thereafter, the club became known as the Hell Fire Club. Its motto was "Do what you will" and meetings are believed to have been little more than orgies, some say that the members even practiced black magic. Many of the caves were used to store wine which no doubt came in very handy for a club meeting. The meetings were reportedly held in the very last cave known as the Inner Temple. This can only be reached by crossing the underground river Styx. Today, it is crossed by a small footbridge but in the days of the Hell Fire Club a small boat was used. There is still a hook in the cave ceiling which was used to hold a large lantern, taken from an inn at Cornhill.

The ghost of Paul Whitehead, a poet and member of the club, is said to haunt the caves and the village. He was responsible for the club's cellar book and on his

49

left his body to science, save for his heart which was placed in an urn at Dashwood's mausoleum. The caves are also reputed to be haunted by another ghost, that of Susie, a serving girl at "The George and Dragon Hotel" in the 18th century. She was murdered in the caves by three local lads and her ghost is said to walk the caves as well as a secret tunnel to "The George and Dragon", where she is known as the White Lady. There are many stories referring to a secret passage from the caves to "The George and Dragon", including a rhyme which has all but been forgotton. Although many attempts have been made, the tunnel has never been found.

A visit to the caves is a must. Even with electric light they are dark and keeping your footing is an adventure in itself. "West Wycombe House", home to the Dashwood's, is also worth a visit, particularly the grounds which are quite magnificent. I recommend however, that you visit the house after the walk, as to do it justice will take several hours. The village although an architectural museum, is somewhat spoilt by the busy A40 which passes through it. The National Trust owned pub, "The Old Plough", is a delightfully rustic place in which to enjoy a drink and the historic coaching inn, "The George and Dragon", which originally dates from the 14th century, also comes highly recommended. There is also "The Swan", a cosy pub which features as part of our recommended accommodation.

There are many paths leading up the hill to the mausoleum, our next destination, but perhaps the easiest way is to retrace your steps to rejoin the walk where you diverted to visit West Wycombe.

Our route if not visiting West Wybcome, is right along the lane and after approximately twenty paces, left onto an unmarked path which leads uphill to shortly pass through some wooden rails and arrive at open hillside. Keep to the path which bends gently left heading for the mausoleum and as you stop for a breather (which undoubtedly you will!), you will enjoy superb views behind to the other side of the valley and High Wycombe. The path soon comes out to the right of the mausoleum which with its excellent views is a perfect place to stop for a rest. Here, in addition to High Wycombe, you will also gain views over West Wycombe Park, complete with lakes and the river Wye which runs through the grounds.

The Dashwood Mausoleum (OS. 828949 Map 175) *dominates the village and the countryside around. It sits six hundred feet high on the site of an old iron age hill fort built by a Celtic tribe under the Chieftain, Heafer. The mausoleum was constructed between the years 1763 and 1765 with monies from the will of Lord Melcombe, who before his death was a member of the Hell Fire Club. Hexagonal in shape with tuscan columns and great arches, the mausoleum is said to have been inspired by Constantine's Arch in Rome. The tomb at the centre is that of Lady Dispencer. Set in niches on the walls are urns reserved for the hearts of members of the Hell Fire Club, although only one heart was ever placed here, that of Paul Whitehead. In later years Whitehead's heart became a great tourist attraction and was regularly removed from the urn and displayed to visitors. It was eventually stolen in 1829, perhaps the reason for Mr. Whitehead's hauntings!*

From the mausoleum, continue ahead along a concrete path which leads through the churchyard, to shortly arrive at the front of the church of St. Lawrence.

The Church of St. Lawrence (OS. 828949 Map 175) *is identifiable for miles around by its huge golden ball on top of the tower. The ball is said to be a copy of the "Ball of Fortune" in Venice which Dashwood visited during his Grand Tour. The ball* can reportedly hold up to ten men and from a porthole in the ball, Sir Francis used to signal by heliograph to his friend John Norris at Camberley, where he in turn had erected a copy of the same golden ball. For a small fee, you can climb the tower to visit the ball but unfortunately, whenever I have tried the church has always been locked.

The church itself is of medieval origin but the alterations carried out by Sir Francis make this period unrecognisable. Instead of a traditional simple nave there is now a richly decorated hall, fashioned in the style of the Temple of Bel at Palmyia.

To continue, facing the front of the church (the tower) in the direction of the mausoleum, turn left to leave the churchyard via a wooden gate. This takes you into a car park which, depending on the time of year, may be wonderfully silent or very busy and noisy. Continue ahead along the left hand perimeter of the car park heading for a house at the far side, "Windyhaugh". There are fabulous views left here. On nearing "Windyhaugh", turn left along a track which passes to the left of the house and after a short distance, pass through a wooden gate.

After the gate, stay on the track which now runs along the top of the hill to virtually lead us back to our starting point. Much of the way is through woodland but at points you will pass through clearings and fields where you are rewarded with yet more excellent views. After some distance the track forks and you should take the right hand fork to maintain your route ahead. Later, ignore a crossing track to continue ahead. Shortly after, the track draws parallel with Bradenham and the trees give way on the right to allow superb views over the village. This is probably the best view of the manor and its magnificent grounds and is also a good point at which to stop and rest before our final descent to perhaps our final resting place, "The Red Lion", at Bradenham!

Pass through a kissing gate and continue ahead until you arrive at the newly restored "Nobles Farm". Almost opposite the farm entrance, take a narrow path right marked by a white arrow and follow this down the side of the wooded Averingdown. As you descend you have further views over Bradenham village, though take care not to pay too much attention to these or you may find

St Botolphs Church

yourself at the bottom of the hill much sooner than expected! As you near the bottom of the hill the path leaves the wood and continues through an area of natural open grassland, a mass of wild flowers and butterflies in summer.

Maintain your descent to meet and cross a stile and thereafter, walk diagonally right across the centre of a long narrow field. At the far side, go over another stile to cross a railway line, taking care as you do so, to meet and cross a third stile into another field. Cross the field and pass through a kissing gate the other side to arrive at the main road, the A4010, once more, in front of the entrance to "Manor Farm". Cross the road and turn right to reach our final pub, "The Red Lion", a free house, where if your timing is right you can enjoy a well earned drink - a perfect end to what I hope has been a perfect day.

From the pub, follow the road into Bradenham village, our starting point, where if you haven't already booked your bed at the Youth Hostel, now may be a good time to join!

ACCOMMODATION

The Swan Inn, West Wycombe. Tel: 0494 527031

On the walk, accommodation is in an historic pub at the National Trust village of West Wycombe.

The White House, Widmer End. Tel: 0494 712221

Approximately one and a half miles from the walk, accommodation is in a self contained suite attached to a house converted from three 17th century cottages.

Youth Hostel, Bradenham YHA, Bradenham. Tel: 0494 56 2929

On the walk, the hostel is in a converted Victorian school at the edge of the village green. It is only a few minutes walk to the village pub, "The Red Lion", making this an ideal place to stay if you are on a budget.

Camping and Caravanning, Gibbons Farm, Horsleys Green. Tel: 0494 482385

Approximately four miles from the walk, this is a small site in an area of outstanding natural beauty. It is open to Camping and Caravanning Club members only. For membership details, tel. 0203 694995.

THE GREAT GORING GRAPPLE

Distance: 12½ miles (20.5 km)

Time: Allow approximately 6½ hours

Map: Ordnance Survey Landranger Maps 174/175

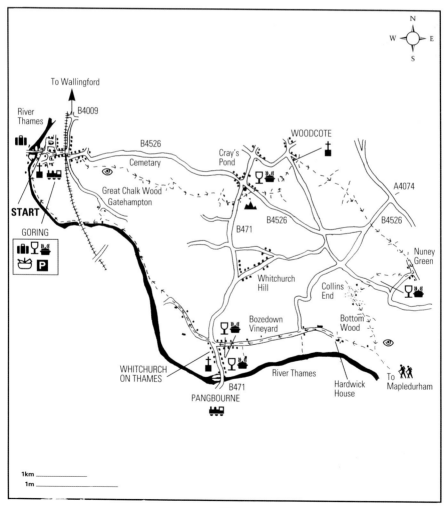

Walk Summary

This is a superb walk taking in all the best features of the Chilterns and in particular, some magnificent beech woodland. Starting from the historic village of Goring, the walk climbs the side of the Thames valley to traverse several miles of traditional Chiltern beech wood. It then makes a sudden and dramatic descent back into the Thames valley, with the last few miles following the river back to Goring. The highlight of the walk is a spectacular and little known view over the Thames, worth more than just a few minutes pause.

Start - OS. 599808 Map 174

The walk starts from the famous "Ye Miller of Mansfield" pub at Goring on Thames. Goring is on or close to several main roads and all the following roads lead directly or indirectly to the village. The B4009 or A329 from Wallingford, the B4526 which can be joined from the A4074 near Reading, the A417 from Harwell, the B4009 from Newbury and the A329 from Reading which can also be joined via the A340, the easiest route from the M4 (junction 12).

There is a pay and display public car park at Goring as well as street parking, though this is probably easier just across the bridge over the Thames at Streatley. An alternative start can be made from Mapledurham which adds just over a mile to the walk but makes for an exciting finish. Goring has a railway station which is on the line that connects Reading with Oxford and therefore, has a frequent service.

THE GREAT GORING GRAPPLE

It is not often that a walk starts from such pleasant surroundings, but at Goring we are spoilt without effort. The only downside is that many other people also recognise Goring's charms and in summer especially, the village can be crowded with people seemingly nervous to explore further than the bridge and river bank!

Goring on Thames (OS. 600808 Map 174/175) is at one of the oldest crossroads in Europe, for here the ancient Icknield Way and Ridgeway converge to cross another major highway, the river Thames. The waters of the Thames were, before man started building weirs and locks, particularly shallow at this point and a ford presented the only safe crossing for miles. Consequently, Goring became a place of some importance and witnessed people both friendly and hostile, as successive races battled to control the thoroughfare. Today, the surrounding countryside is littered with remains from the various Celtic, Roman, Saxon and Danish armies.

With the arrival of the Romans, the ford was upgraded to a causeway which remained in use until the 17th century, when the more important requirements of river traffic led to the building of the first lock and weir. After this, the only way across the river was by ferry which, by all accounts, was unsafe and unreliable. A tragedy in 1674 saw almost fifty people drowned when their overcrowded ferry, returning to Streatley from the Goring fair, capsized. Despite this, the first bridge was not constructed until 1838. The present bridge was built in 1923.

From the centre of the bridge you perhaps gain the best views of Goring and its neighbour, Streatley. The "Swan Diplomat Hotel" on the Streatley bank, arguably belongs to Goring as it was granted to the nuns of Goring in the 13th century. The hotel was once owned by the entertainer, Danny La Rue. The Goring bank apart from an old mill beside the bridge, is a show piece for Edwardian architecture. Grand houses, some with elaborate boathouses, line the bank in a shameless display of affluence. Incidentally, the old mill by the bridge is the main feature in an unfinished painting by Turner.

Long before the Edwardians, Goring's Norman Lord, Robert D'Oyley, built the fine church we see today. Escaping the enthusiastic attention of the Victorians, the church remains virtually unaltered and is thus a fine example of Norman architecture. It is perhaps best viewed from the river bank at the end of the walk. Inside, the church contains one of the oldest bells in the country, cast in 1290. There are also a number of interesting brasses.

In the 12th century a priory was formed by nuns adjacent to the church. In the same century, an Augustinian priory was formed at the hamlet of Cleeve (now part of Goring), just one and a half miles away. A tunnel was said to have connected the two, though it has never been discovered. Both priories were dissolved under Henry VIII.

Goring is worth exploring further than the river bank, having many old and unspoilt buildings. "Ferry House", once "Ferry Cottage", was the holiday home of Oscar Wilde and later the home of "Bomber" Harris. "Ye Miller of Mansfield", our starting point, is a fine 17th century inn. Goring's oldest hostelry is "The Catherine Wheel", Brakspear's, which is near the entrance to the public car park. Another fine pub is "The John Barleycorn", also Brakspear's. Goring also has a number of tea rooms and cafes and for those who prefer eating in the hills, there is a general stores from where provisions can be purchased.

From the ivy clad "Ye Miller of Mansfield", walk up the main road, away from the Thames, and follow it past shops ignoring all turnings off to go over the railway bridge and arrive at a crossroads. Turn right at the crossroads in the direction of the sign for Cray's Pond and Reading, and after approximately twenty metres, turn left onto another road in front of "The Queens Arms", Morrells, still following the signs for Cray's Pond and Reading.

Continue along the road for approximately forty metres and then turn right into a relatively modern residential road, Whitehills Green. Follow Whitehills Green round to the left and at the end of the cul-de-sac, where there is a small paved roundabout, bear right to leave the road by taking a narrow hedged path between gardens. This leads to a stile which you should cross into a recreation field where you are immediately rewarded with views to your right to the shapely hills the other side of the Thames.

Bear diagonally left across the recreation field heading for the far left hand corner and on reaching the latter, go over a stile and turn left to follow the left hand perimeter of another field, going uphill. As you climb you gain excellent views behind over the Thames valley and easily visible is Brunel's four arch bridge, taking the London to Bristol railway line over the Thames. The bridge also marks the last stretch of our walk today.

At the far side of the field go over a stile and continue ahead along the left hand perimeter of the next field, with Great Chalk Wood, our next destination, coming into view ahead to your right. On your left, though difficult to see because of the thick hedgerow, is Goring cemetary. At the far side of the field turn right to continue following the field perimeter round and descending into a valley. At the bottom of the valley you will also arrive at the next corner of the field and here you should go over a stile ahead, to follow a prominent path ahead through scrub.

After approximately twenty metres, go over another stile and follow the path ahead through Great Chalk Wood. Keep to the main path through the wood, ignoring all turnings off, following the regularly spaced arrows painted on tree trunks. The path leads steadily uphill and after bearing gently left, levels off and at the same time, becomes more of a track. Later, it meets a crossing track which you should ignore to continue straight on. A short time after, a marked footpath (white arrow) joins from the right which you should also ignore, to continue for a further twenty metres where the track bends sharp right. Here you should leave it by passing through a small gate on the left in the direction of a blue bridleway arrow. Take care not to miss it.

The bridleway leads downhill between banks and after a short distance, bends right to meet a crossing track. Go over the crossing track and follow a prominent path ahead which in turn follows the line of a field, somewhat hidden behind a mature hedge on your left. The path leads gently uphill and eventually arrives at a gate through which you should pass, to continue along a fenced path between fields. After a short distance, pass through a second gate and continue ahead through a garden to soon join a tarmac drive to the beautiful "Bottom Farmhouse" on your left **(OS. 629633 Map 175).**

Maintain your route by following the drive away from the farmhouse to soon pass some stables on your left, after which the drive becomes a simple farm track. Continue ahead following the track uphill through woodland and at the far side of the wood, ignore a prominent crossing path, keeping to the track which now runs between fields. A short time on, the track becomes tarmacked and again you should continue ahead passing between a couple of desirable properties, before eventually arriving at a "T" junction in the form of the B471. Cross the road and pass through a gap in the hedge the other side to then bear diagonally left across the centre of a field, heading for the far left hand corner and ignoring a path running round the field perimeter.

On leaving the field at the corner you will arrive at a road, the B4526, beside a sign for "The Oratory Preparatory School". A short detour left along the B4526 will bring you to Cray's Pond, a small hamlet encircling a pond and crossroads. Here you will find your first chance for refreshments in the form of "The White Lion", Morland.

Cross the road and turn right the other side along a path through a wood which runs parallel with the road. After approximately twenty metres the path bends left through the centre of the wood, in the direction of a public footpath sign beside the road on your right. As before, keep to the main path, marked by painted white arrows, ignoring all turnings off. As you progress, look out for a quite distinct bank in the undergrowth on your left. This is thought to be the remains of a medieval enclosure. Later, the path arrives at a crossing track onto which you should turn right and after approximately twenty paces, leave it to join a narrow path on your left, marked by a white arrow, thereby maintaining your original direction.

After a short distance, the path enters an area of mature beech woodland and becomes a little less defined. Here it is doubly important you look carefully for those white arrows. Further on, you will arrive at a "T" junction in the form of another footpath, marked by white arrows on the trunk of a tree ahead. Turn left here, following the new footpath, again guided by the white arrows and when the path forks (marked by white arrows) a short distance on, take the right hand path.

This path continues in a straight line through the beech wood to shortly pass through another medieval enclosure (look out for the banks). Later, it passes to the right of some pits and just after these, through the trees on your right, you will see a lovely old farmhouse. Continue to follow the white arrows to eventually arrive at a lane in front of an old methodist chapel **(OS. 647810 Map 175)**. Turn right along the lane passing in front of the chapel and after approximately fifteen metres, turn left onto a signposted footpath. This leads through woodland known as Birchen Copse where, at the time of writing, there are no white arrows to guide your way. However, the path is fairly well used and easy to follow and if you want additional reassurance, some houses which mark the outskirts of the village of Woodcote on your left, should be visible throughout.

After approximately fifty metres you will arrive at a crossing path beside a small pit on your right, possibly an old saw pit (see "Follow the Red Brick Road"). Turn left here, now being guided once more by white arrows, heading for the houses of Woodcote. After approximately twenty metres, you will arrive at a somewhat confusing junction of paths, all marked by white arrows. Take the second path on the right almost going back on yourself, which follows the line of a field on your left. In winter when the trees are bare there are lovely views left towards Checkendon.

Eventually, the fields on your left give way to the wood and at the same time, you will meet a wide crossing track, marked by white arrows, which you should ignore to carry straight on. Once again, your way through the wood is along a well defined path, reassuringly marked by a number of white arrows on tree trunks. After some distance, you will arrive at a crossing path, also marked by white arrows, and you should go straight over this to continue ahead. Sometime on, you will meet a marked path (white arrows) off to your right which you should ignore, as before, to carry straight on. Soon after this, the path you are following bends left and then right to meet another path onto which you should turn right, still following the white arrows, to eventually meet the 20th century again in the form of a main road, the B4526, **(OS. 663800 Map 175)**.

Cross the road and take a signposted bridleway the other side, signposted to Nuney Green, to continue your passage through the wood. I am sure I do not need to remind you, but continue to follow the white arrows. Later, fields cut into the wood on your left and the bridleway follows the line of these, though not through the fields themselves. As the fields end, you should ignore first a marked path off to the right and then another on the left, to carry straight on. Shortly after this, the bridleway runs to the right of a long oblong clearing, though in summer this may not be easily visible. (If you find yourself entering the clearing itself, then you will somehow have taken the wrong path and should bear right to rejoin the main route, which is quite prominent and clearly marked by the now familiar white arrows).

As the clearing, if visible, on your left ends you will arrive at a rather gloomy pond. You should bear left here to follow the left hand edge of the pond and follow a path in the direction of the white arrows to pass between the pond on your right and a series of hollows on your left. After the pond, the path which at this point can often be very muddy, continues in a straight line to shortly run between the houses of Nuney Green.

On reaching a track which serves the hamlet of Nuney Green, join it to continue ahead and follow it as it bends right, ignoring another track which carries straight on. The track now becomes an asphalt lane which you should follow between the houses of the hamlet, the last house being a thatched property on the left which looks like something out of a Grimms fairy tale. It has an ornate garage to match! Just after this and on meeting the entrance to "The Firs" on your right, pass through a wooden barrier on the right to follow a bridleway, once again through woodland. This, as before, is marked by white arrows on tree trunks.

Some distance into the wood, the bridleway meets a crossing path onto which you should turn left, still following the white arrows. The path, more a track, leads downhill to traverse a shallow valley covered in tall beech trees and in places, with a very fine rich green grass. At the other side of the valley, ignore a crossing path and continue straight on, in the direction of the white arrows, through the wood to eventually meet a lane. Do not take the signposted footpath the other side of the lane, but turn left instead along the lane to, after approximately thirty metres, arrive at one of the jewels on the walk, "The King Charles Head", a free house **(OS. 664789 Map 175)**.

This lovely pub stands at the edge of the wood offering refreshments to travellers as it has done for centuries. A copy of the original pub sign hangs on the wall with a rhyme recalling a visit by King Charles I. The rhyme also reminds you that stopping at a good pub can help you forget all the troubles in the world, even losing your crown! The pub has a lovely garden where in summer you can enjoy a good barbecue. Indeed, the pub food comes highly recommended and as it is almost all downhill or flat from here, I recommend you try some.

At "The King Charles Head", take a footpath opposite the pub which runs across the centre of a small field, at the end of which you should pass through a gap in the hedge. Thereafter, follow a narrow path through scrub for approximately twenty paces, to then bear right over a stile into a field. Once in the field, turn left and follow the left hand perimeter. When I last walked this way the path was lined with rabbits not easily scared and almost under my feet! At the far side, go over a stile and continue in the same direction across the next field and after approximately twenty metres, pass through a gap in the fence ahead to join a drive belonging to a house on your left.

Follow the drive ahead which runs between fields and the scattered houses of Collins End and on meeting a tarmac lane, turn left to follow it past "Briar Cottage". Soon after, you will pass a lovely old farmhouse on the right, where the lane ends, and you should continue ahead along a gravel track to, a few paces on, arrive at an almost completely unspoilt half timbered cottage. Here you should leave the track to take a narrow path directly ahead, passing to the right of the cottage.

Follow the path downhill through Bottom Wood, at one point passing between some quite steep banks where you will meet steps either side of the path. You should ignore these and carry

Pass to the right of the cottage

58

straight on to reach the bottom of a small wooded valley at which point you should turn left. After approximately twenty paces, turn right (ignoring the track ahead), onto a wide path which leads gently up the other side of the valley. As you progress, the path gradually bends right and levels out, continuing in a straight line through the wood. Later, you should ignore a stepped crossing path to continue until the path forks, marked by a white arrow. (Take care not to miss it).

Take the left hand fork, the path ahead and the less prominent path, to meander through the wood which eventually ends as you arrive at a stile. Cross the stile and follow a path ahead to arrive at open grass hillside, Straw Hill, where you are immediately rewarded with fabulous views across the Thames valley. The view is one you will want to take home with you and I shall not do it an injustice by trying to give a description. Instead, I will simply say - enjoy it!

To continue, go straight down the side of the hill heading for a stile amongst some wooden rails, visible below. At the bottom go over the stile to reach a well used path. A detour left along the path for approximately half a mile will bring you to Mapledurham, with its famous Elizabethan house and water mill. The house is said to have been the model for Kenneth Grahame's "Toad Hall" in his book "Wind in the Willows". It is certainly a magical place and if you do not visit now, I recommend you return to discover it another day.

Our way however, is right to sometime on arrive at a pair of ornate iron gates. Pass through a gap next to the gates to reach a track beside two pretty cottages on your right. Continue ahead along the track, which runs in a straight line, following the line of the Thames on your left. Sometime later, the track forks and you should take the right hand fork, thereby continuing straight on (the left fork is the private drive to "Hardwick House").

Hardwick House (OS. 658778 Map 175). *Tall chimneys and an ornate clock tower just visible above a thick yew hedge, are the only clues that an historic house stands here. A house has stood on this site since the Norman conquest and took its name from the original builder the Norman, Lord de Hardewyke. After the family died out, it was purchased by the Tudor politician and Server to Queen Mary and Queen Elizabeth I, Richard Lybbe. It was Lybbe who built the current house, a house fit to entertain Queen Elizabeth I. In honour of her visit Lybbe had three portraits of her majesty cleverly incorporated into the ceiling decoration of her room.*

During the next century the house welcomed another royal guest, Charles I, who whilst being held captive at Caversham, was allowed to visit the house and partake in a game of bowls. The house was badly damaged during the Civil War but was tastefully restored in its Tudor style.

As the yew hedge on your left ends you will arrive at a junction of tracks where you should ignore all turnings off to carry straight on, now following a tarmac drive. Stay on the drive to sometime later, pass the beautiful "Hardwick Farmhouse" and stables. After the farm, the drive continues between fields where there are some lovely views left across to the Thames. The drive ends after passing between a pair of gatehouses to arrive at a lane. Sometimes on the left here there is a small caravan selling fresh organically grown strawberries, a refreshing treat to revive you on the walk.

Our way is now directly ahead (not right), along the lane until we reach the B471 at Whitchurch on Thames, a distance of just over a mile. Almost half way along, you will pass "Bozedown Home Farm" which has its own vineyard and produces it own wine. The farm is a member of the English Vineyards Association and the wine produced has won a number of international awards. The vineyard is open to the public at weekends for tastings and wine sales, though if you can find a member of staff, they are quite willing to making a sale during the week and I can hardly think of a better souvenir of your adventure. Considering the farm's name and its produce, I am sure I am not the first person to suggest a slight change of name by adding an "o" to make it "Boozedown"!

The lane is normally very quiet and has a wide grass verge along which you can walk and after "Bozedown Home Farm", a hedged path runs above the road on the right. It later descends, on meeting the suburbs of Whitchurch, where you can follow the pavement until you meet the B471 **(OS. 634775 Map 175)**. Here it is possible to make another short detour by following the B471 left into Whitchurch on Thames.

Whitchurch on Thames (OS. 635770 Map 175) *is a lovely and relatively unspoilt Thames-side village. The long attractive main street (also the B471), leads down to the Thames, where one of only two toll bridges left on the river carries you into Pangbourne. Beside the bridge is a lovely old mill dating from Norman times. The church, which can be reached by taking a path beside the mill, is also Norman, though Victorian architects have done their best to disguise this. Buried in the church is Sir Thomas Walysch, wine taster to John O' Gaunt and later to Henry IV, Henry V and Henry VI. For his loyal service in what was a potentially lethal profession, Sir Thomas was presented the manor of Whitchurch. He died a natural death and I am sure, a very happy man.*

Whitchurch has two excellent and very different hostelries. "The Greyhound", Halls Ales, is a traditional pub with a cosy bar, low beamed ceiling and a secluded garden. "The Ferryboat Inn", Morlands, has been tastefully modernised around a boating theme. The menu at "The Ferryboat Inn" is particularly good and imaginative and the pub is also featured in our recommended accommation.

To continue, on arriving at the B471 at Whitchurch, turn right along it. The first stretch is particularly narrow without any pavements, so please take care of the sometimes heavy traffic. After a short distance, you will see a track on the left, signposted as a public bridleway and "To Goring, 3 miles". It is also signposted to "Longacre Farm". Take this to walk between a number of enviable houses, one of which on your left is "Coombe Park", the superb grounds being visible through a wooden fence.

After approximately one mile the track bends left to go to "Hartslock Farm", where you should leave it to carry straight on along a signposted public bridleway. This initially descends via steps and then becomes a narrow path leading uphill between fields. It soon levels out after passing between a few elegant beech trees and some distance on, meets and meanders through Hartslock Wood, at points coming quite close to the Thames.

The path later forks and you should take the left hand fork to follow a fence on your left, which protects walkers from a cliff edge. From here you are afforded some excellent views over the river. Soon after, the bridleway gradually descends to virtually meet and follow the Thames. Further on, the path passes an old pill box, a grim reminder of less pleasant times and some distance after this, you should look out for a marked footpath (yellow arrow) off to the right. This, the footpath just mentioned, is not part of our route, but is another detour I recommend by going over a stile to Hartslock Hill. This is an area of chalk grassland, a nature reserve run by BBONT, and a lovely hillside spot at which to stop and enjoy yet more good views over the Thames and the Goring Gap. You will need to retrace your steps to rejoin our route.

Returning to our route, continue ahead now walking between fields. After a short distance and as you approach the few houses at Gatehampton, just visible ahead, take a fenced path left marked as a permissive path (white arrow in a green circle). Take care not to miss it. The path leads between fields, at the far side of which you should continue ahead over a footbridge to meet the river Thames beside "Ferry Cottage" on your left. The cottage marks the spot where a ferry once connected the tow path on opposing banks. Turn right to follow the Thames up river to later, after passing through a wooden gate, arrive at an open grass area in front of a large four arch bridge over the Thames.

Brunel's Bridge

The Lost Hamlet of Gatehampton (OS. 606796 Map 175). *The graceful, some might say ugly, arched railway bridge built by Brunel, roughly marks the spot of the lost hamlet of Gatehampton. There has been a settlement here as far back as the Stone Age and the Romans later built a villa on the site. After the Romans the hamlet prospered, and by the time of the Norman conquest, included a fulling mill (a mill which cleansed wool) and a fishery. After going into decline, the hamlet apparently came to an end in 1515, when the Lord of the manor evicted the fourteen residents, probably on economic grounds. Today, the site of the lost hamlet is our recommended campsite.*

Pass beneath the bridge, after which we follow the river Thames all the way back to Goring. As you follow the river through a succession of fields, you have a lovely view right of the beginning of the walk. After passing in front of a beautifully restored boathouse, the first houses of Goring will come into view on your right. Later, after passing a couple more boathouses, the famous bridge over the Thames which connects Streatley with Goring, comes into view. Just before reaching the bridge, there is an attractive view right across a mill pond to Goring church. Do not pass under the bridge, but turn right instead immediately before it, following a path over the mill race and passing in front of the old mill. Continue to soon meet the main road through Goring, the B4009, and follow this ahead to arrive back at "Ye Miller of Mansfield". You can now relax and idle away the hours by playing Pooh Sticks from the bridge or by celebrating in a local hostelry, a difficult choice!

ACCOMMODATION

Ye Miller of Mansfield, Goring. Tel: 0491 872829
On the walk, this ivy clad inn with its low beams and open fires is the perfect place to stay and relax after your walk. The bedrooms are all well furnished and have good facilities.

The Ferryboat Inn, Whitchurch on Thames. Tel: 0734 842161
Virtually on the walk, this is a recently refurbished inn with the decor having a boating theme. The rooms are excellent and you need not leave the inn to enjoy a well deserved meal.

Youth Hostel, Streatley YHA, Streatley. Tel: 0491 872278
Virtually on the walk, the recently refurbished Streatley hostel now offers small family rooms as well as the normal dorms we all know. The hostel itself is a large Victorian house only a few paces from "The Bull Inn".

Camping and Caravanning, Gatehampton Farm, Goring. Tel: 0491 872894
On the walk, this is an informal site on the bank of the river Thames. Facilities are minimal but then that is the beauty of its location. A pleasant walk takes you to the attractions of Goring centre.

THE HAMPDEN HOWLER

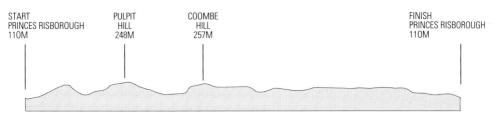

Distance: 13 miles (21 km)

Time: Allow approximately 6½ hours

Map: Ordnance Survey Landranger Map 165

THE HAMPDEN HOWLER · SOUTH CHILTERNS

START PRINCES RISBOROUGH 110M	PULPIT HILL 248M	COOMBE HILL 257M	FINISH PRINCES RISBOROUGH 110M

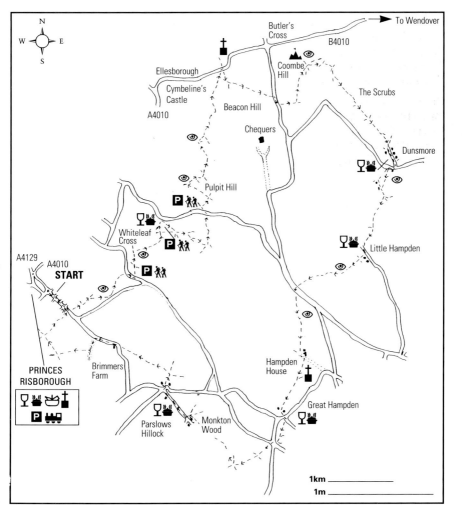

Walk Summary

The Hampden Howler explores the escarpment above Whiteleaf visiting some of the Chilterns most famous landmarks. The beginning of the walk, in part, follows the popular Ridgeway trail before heading south west to Great Hampden. The finale is a magnificent descent from the wooded Windsor Hill through a sweeping curve of fields to Princes Risborough. Why the Hampden Howler? The walk is fairly testing and has more than its fair share of steep ascents and I have no doubt that on at least one of these you will be howling for my blood!

Start - OS. 809034 Map 165

The walk starts from the roundabout on the A4010 opposite a modern development called "Tower Court" at Princes Risborough. As a guide, a road other than the A4010 from the roundabout is signposted to Horns Lane car park, it is also close to Budgens supermarket. Horns Lane car park is restricted to no more than two hours parking (except Sundays), though street parking is possible close by and there is a long term car park near the town's Norman church.

Getting to Princes Risborough is fairly easy as apart from the A4010, the town is also served by the A4129 from Thame. If travelling along the M40, turn off at junction 6 and take the B4009 in the direction of the signs for Chinnor and Princes Risborough. Continue until you meet the A4129 at Longwick (a roundabout) and turn right to follow the A4129 into Princes Risborough. Princes Risborough also has a railway station though the Sunday service is somewhat infrequent.

There are several possible alternative starts. They are the car park for Whiteleaf Hill (OS. 822039), the public car park at "The Plough" pub (OS. 826045) and the parking area for Pulpit Hill (OS. 834046), though finding them is easier if you have local knowledge.

THE HAMPDEN HOWLER

Despite some modern development, Princes Risborough remains a mainly rural and attractive town with more than its fair share of pretty corners. These are worth searching out as is the town's history, but bearing in mind the climbs in store for you I suggest you conserve your energy for your impending adventure.

To start, from the roundabout at "Tower Court", take New Road which is signposted to Horns Lane car park. Follow the road uphill past the car park, ignoring any turnings off, until you meet a national speed limit sign (black diagonal line in a white circle) on the outskirts of the town. Here you should turn left onto a crossing track marked as the Upper Icknield Way and also signposted as the Ridgeway. You are now treading a route which has seen centuries of travel (see "Taming the Lions"). The track, at first, runs between houses and then after a short distance arable fields appear on your right. Keep to the track until you see a Ridgeway signpost pointing to a gap in the hedge on your right. Leave the track at this point and follow the Ridgeway, passing through the gap in the hedge, into a field where you should continue ahead along the right hand field perimeter. Ahead to your left now are the best views on the walk of the mysterious Whiteleaf Cross cut into Whiteleaf Hill, the summit of which is our next destination.

At the far side of the field, pass through a gap in the hedge beside a derelict stile and maintain your route uphill, following a fence on your right through an area of natural chalk grassland. The climb is fairly steep and taking the occasional breather allows you to admire the views behind over Princes Risborough. Further up, go over a stile and follow a well used path uphill through scrub. After going over a crossing path the way becomes quite steep and steps have been provided to help you and to avoid erosion. Eventually, the path breaks free of the scrub and your efforts are rewarded with some magnificent views behind over the Vale of Aylesbury. On a clear day you can even see the cooling towers of Didcot Power Station.

After going over a stile, continue ahead, still going uphill, across the centre of a field. Do not make the common mistake of bearing left. You will now find yourself walking along something of a spur which affords more glorious views, especially on your right, to Lodge Hill and Bledlow Ridge, featured in "Taming the Lions". As you progress, you will meet and follow the field's right hand perimeter, the other side of which is a narrow lane (do not join it). Soon after this you will arrive at a stile. Do not cross the stile but turn left instead to continue following the field perimeter in the direction of a Ridgeway signpost. (Do not take the path across the centre of the field). You should now be walking between a wood on your right and the old field perimeter, marked by a thin line of trees and bushes, on your left.

After a short distance, you will meet a stile ahead with a yellow arrow and white acorn. Cross this to thereafter follow a semi-tarmacked path ahead which soon bends left to meet a lane. Follow the lane ahead and after approximately thirty paces, turn left onto a track signposted as the Ridgeway. The track leads round the Whiteleaf Hill car park and picnic area (alternative start), and then continues in a straight line along the top of Whiteleaf Hill. Keep to the track and therefore the Ridgeway, ignoring all turnings off including signposted ones, to eventually arrive at a large grass clearing which marks the summit of Whiteleaf Hill and the site of the mysterious cross.

The Whiteleaf Cross (OS. 822040 Map 165) *can be viewed from above by bearing left across the clearing to reach a low single bar fence above the cross. The Whiteleaf Cross and its neighbour, the Bledlow Cross on Wain Hill, are the only two turf cut crosses in Britain. The Bledlow Cross almost certainly dates from the 13th century but the date and origin of the Whiteleaf Cross is still a matter of debate. One theory is that it was cut by medieval monks from Monks Risborough, though this is unlikely as there would probably be a record of it and the practice of monks cutting chalk figures anywhere else is virtually unknown. Another theory is that it was cut to guide travellers along the Icknield Way, though this too is highly unlikely.*

The most popular and most probable theory is that the cross was once an ancient fertility sign, later converted to a cross by early Christians. The practice of absorbing pagan symbols into the Christian church was common and deliberate, designed to help the pagan Britons accept the new religion. The church, because of the Virgin birth and its Christian morals, found it a little harder to accept the pagans' direct approach to fertility worship. This made things difficult for the early Christians as fertility rights and worship formed the very basis of pagan religion.

Eostre, the pagan goddess of fertility, was represented on earth by the hare. A celebration of Eostre was held each spring with a collection of eggs from the fields which the pagans believed had been laid by the hare and were therefore, a gift from Eostre. The eggs were in fact the eggs of a bird, the lap wing. The early Christians incorporated the date of the pagan Eostre spring festival to celebrate the resurrection of Christ. They even celebrated it under the name of the pagans' goddess, Eostre, which today has been corrupted to Easter. Although not accepted by the Christian church, the pagans' celebration of the egg continued and remains today in the form of the Easter egg.

The hare was the most revered symbol of fertility and was considered by the pagans as a holy animal barred from being hunted. The early Christians simply could not incorporate such a distinct pagan symbol into their religion and centuries on, people caught worshipping the hare were burned at the stake as witches. The Christians also blatantly made fun of the hare, comparing it with the humble and hunted rabbit. They did this by dressing captured hares in silly clothes for people to laugh at, the origin of the Easter bunny as we know it today.

Considering the lengths to which the early Christians went in cleverly adopting pagan fertility symbols and traditions, it is quite feasible that the same thing happened here at Whiteleaf, turning an ancient fertility symbol into a cross. There are some excellent views to be had from Whiteleaf Hill, worth more than a few minutes rest, during which time you can form your own theory on the origin of the cross.

To continue, with your back to the cross, take the path ahead, still following the Ridgeway, to shortly pass through a kissing gate beside a Buckinghamshire County Council sign for Whiteleaf Hill (as a guide, the Ridgeway points right as you arrive at the grass clearing). After the kissing gate, continue ahead along a prominent path through Giles Wood to, after a short distance, arrive at a small grass area beneath a number of low beech trees. There is also a low stone post with the familiar white acorn of the Ridgeway. This is another lovely place to stop with more good views, this time across a densely wooded valley.

After the grass clearing the path descends quite steeply (ignore any turnings off) and being mainly chalk, can be very slippery. Sometime on, you will arrive at a junction of paths and tracks where you should maintain your route along the Ridgeway, which is signposted, to continue your descent following a fence on your left. After a short distance, the path meets a track onto which you should turn left to almost immediately after, arrive at a metal gate and stile. Go over the stile and continue ahead to join another track which you should follow downhill to arrive at "The Plough" pub, Benskins. "The Plough" is the only pub on the Ridgeway making it a very popular place to stop for walkers and the publican has placed a number of benches on a small green opposite, where outdoor types like us can enjoy a drink without having to remove boots and muddy clothing. Apart from good beer the pub offers some excellent home cooked food.

From "The Plough" it is possible to take a short cut by following the Ridgeway until you arrive at an iron field gate and kissing gate **(OS. 834054)**, where you can rejoin the official route by taking a path left. This part of the Ridgeway is extremely popular and becoming very worn and for the Hampden Howler therefore, I have decided to take a different route which explores the iron age hill fort on Pulpit Hill. To do this, with your back to "The Plough", take a signposted footpath right, also marked as a circular walk. This involves going over a stile beside a pair of gates before following a track ahead, passing to the left of a car park (alternative start - **OS. 826045**). The track runs along the bottom of a valley which shortly divides, where there are a number of paths leading off in all directions. You should take the track (not a path) ahead which forks left to soon pass between an old set of gate posts beside a stile. On one of the gate posts is a yellow footpath arrow.

The track gradually bends left continuing to follow the bottom of the valley and then, after a short distance, bends sharp right up the side of the valley in the direction of a yellow footpath arrow. You should ignore another track which continues ahead along the bottom of the valley. Approximately half way up, look out for a marked (yellow arrow) narrow footpath on your left (take care not to miss it), and take this to continue your climb up the valley side. As you climb you are afforded some good views behind, down the valley, to the Vale of Aylesbury.

On reaching an area of mature beech wood, the path levels out and from here you are guided by white arrows to eventually meet a sunken crossing path. Go over a low stile to join the crossing path and thereafter, turn left along it, ignoring a marked footpath on your right. You should now follow the path which is fenced and often very muddy, to eventually meet a lane (**OS. 834045**). Cross the lane and join a signposted bridleway the other side, a track, and follow this passing behind a small parking area and as the latter ends, where you will meet a one bar gate ahead, turn right onto a narrow path which leads steeply uphill. Ignore all turnings off until you reach a crossing track near the top of the hill, marked by white arrows.

Turn left along the track which, as a guide, runs parallel with a line of beech trees growing on a low bank on your right. Later and as the line of beech trees begins to break up, you will see a much steeper bank and ditch on your right. These are part of the old ramparts of an iron age hill fort. Shortly after this, the track bends right and on meeting the edge of the hill, forks. You should keep right along the edge of the hill to soon walk along the top of one of the old ramparts. A short distance on, a break in the trees allows for a lovely view left to Great Kimble church, a good moment to pause and for me to talk about the hill fort.

Pulpit Hill Fort, 248m (OS. 833050 Map 165) *was a small but well fortified iron age (Celtic) hill fort. It was protected by a double bank and ditch with the entrance close to where we joined the ramparts at the edge of the hill. There is little evidence of occupation and it is likely that the fort acted as a temporary refuge, should the local tribe find themselves under attack. From the evidence of the double ramparts attacks were probably quite frequent. When the fort was at its height the banks and ditches would have formed a defence tens of feet in height, strengthened by a high wooden stockade. At the entrance it is likely that there would have been a pair of strong and well protected wooden gates.*

A favourite weapon of the Celts was the sling, particularly useful in fending off an attack on a fort. Amongst the Celtic prize spoils of war were their opponents' heads which would be hacked from the bodies of their victims and errected on poles around the fort to warn off potential attackers. It is believed the heads of important enemies were preserved in cedar oil and kept at the Chieftain's house to be shown off to visitors. Try and imagine the fort in its hey-day. There were no trees to hide it and the fort on top of such a steep hill with its formidable ramparts, stockade and severed heads on full display, must have made the most determined attacker think twice!

To continue, maintain your route along the edge of the hill, later ignoring a marked footpath (white arrow) off to your right. Soon after this, the path forks and you should take the right hand fork, the more prominent path, to shortly pass through an old fence and soon after, a low bank before meeting a wide crossing path. Go over the crossing path following a narrow path ahead, marked by a white arrow, and a short distance on, cross a stile and continue following the path ahead, which soon after breaks free of the wood coming out onto open grass hillside.

Go over a narrow crossing path and continue ahead, now going downhill, to arrive at another crossing path onto which you should turn right. A few paces on, the crossing path bends left where you should ignore another path ahead to your right. After this, the path continues to bend left to eventually meet the Ridgeway at an iron field gate and kissing gate (**OS. 834054**). If from "The Plough" pub you have followed the Ridgeway, this is where you rejoin the Hampden Howler.

Do not join the Ridgeway but cross it, going over a stile the other side (if you have followed the Ridgeway, this is on your left), to thereafter follow a grass path which in turn follows the line of a field on your right. When the field perimeter bends gently right, you should maintain your route straight on, going up a grass knoll which overlooks a very steep sided valley known as Kimble Warren. The valley was formed by the melting of a huge glacier at the end of the ice age. Similar valleys (but not quite as dramatic) can be found all over the Chilterns, they are commonly known as "dry valleys", as they are rarely fed by a spring.

At the other side of the valley is another grass knoll known as Chequer's Knap. The knoll is probably man-made and very ancient, "knap" being a Celtic word for "hill". Chequer's Knap together with your current position, would have made excellent look-out posts for the fort on Pulpit Hill or even Cymbeline's Castle, passed later lower down the slope.

From your lofty viewpoint, join a prominent grass path right, leading away from the valley and descending to reach a stile which you should cross into a field. Once in the field, the path immediately forks and you should take the left hand fork to shortly arrive at a wide track at the other side of the field. Turn left along the track and go over a stile beside a gate, thereafter continuing ahead to a few paces on, meet a tarmac drive. Go straight across the drive and continue ahead along a track the other side, taking heed of the green signs stating "Private. No Admittance". These denote that we are walking through the grounds of "Chequers", the official country residence of the Prime Minister. "Chequers" was donated to the nation in 1909 by Arthur Lee, M.P.

The track you are following now leads through the woods of "Chequers" estate and shortly arrives at a field, where directly ahead of you is the oddly shaped Beacon Hill also known as Cymbeline's Mount. The track bears left across the centre of the field where there are yet more good views to be enjoyed to your left over the now familiar Vale of Aylesbury. At the far side, follow a path down some steps and continue along the steep side of a lush valley, known as Ellesborough Warren, to reach a stile. Go over the stile and follow the path along the left hand perimeter of a field with the slopes of Beacon Hill rising sharply above you to your right.

When the field perimeter bends left you should leave it to carry straight on along a prominent path which runs along the side of the hill. Lower down the slope to your left, in the next field, are some old earth works known as Cymbeline's Castle.

i **Cymbeline's Castle (OS. 833064 Map 165)** *is so-called because it is believed to have once been a stronghold of the Celtic King Cymbeline or Cunobelinus. This assumption appears to have been based on the fact that a gold coin bearing the head of Cymbeline was found nearby.*

Cymbeline was the celebrated King of the Catevellauni tribe during the 1st century. Before the Roman invasions they held roughly the area known today as the Midlands. Cymbeline's father, Cassivellannus, was instrumental in agreeing a treaty with Rome, after which the Roman forces left Briton. Briton may well have been left alone after this, but with the departure of the Romans, Cassivellannus saw an opportunity to expand his tribal empire and attacked the Celtic Trinovantes who held part of the east coast and inland to St. Albans and London. The Trinovantes who had relied mainly upon the Romans for their security, were easily defeated and the new capital for the Catevellaunis was established at Colchester.

Cymbeline was even more aggressive than his father and waged war on other tribes and it was not long before he controlled what is now known as Kent, as well as the Cotswolds and parts of Wiltshire. After his death in AD40, two of his sons, Togodumnus and Caradoc, continued their father's crusade. Things almost came to a head when the King of the beleagured Attrebates fled to Rome for help. Rome however, ignored his requests for protection but when the now confident Caradoc demanded from Rome the extradition of another exile, Verica, Briton could no longer be ignored. In AD43, the Romans launched the invasion of Briton which was to start a new era, but that is another story.

Whether Cymbeline really ever occupied the fort below is very doubtful, in fact it is far more likely to have been constructed by the Romans. In the 18th century, the castle was known as Belinus's Castle. As I mentioned earlier, it would appear it was only named after Cymbeline after the discovery of a coin. It is also doubtful whether Great Kimble is derived from the name Cymbeline. Great Kimble instead is probably of Saxon origin and means "royal bell-shaped hill". This possibly refers to Chequer's Knap or perhaps even Pulpit Hill. The "royal" connection could of course refer to Cymbeline, in which case if you believe in the Cymbeline theory, Great Kimble becomes "royal Cymbeline" which also makes sense.

The earth work is, not surprisingly, steeped in legend and it is said that if you run round the castle seven times, you will conjure up the devil.

As you skirt the hill, the church tower at Ellesborough comes into view ahead and marks our next destination. The path soon begins to descend (where to your right you will see the monument at the top of Coombe Hill), to reach a stile at the far corner of the field which you should cross to follow a narrow path between bushes before arriving at another field. Go straight across the centre of the field heading for the far right hand corner and for Ellesborough church, now dominating the view ahead. At the far corner of the field, pass through a kissing gate to meet a lane where it is worth stopping for a moment to look back at the distinct outline of Beacon Hill.

Turn right along the lane and after a few paces, just after a bus stop, turn right onto a track (marked as a public footpath). First though, it would be a shame not to visit Ellesborough church.

Ellesborough Church (OS. 837068 Map 165) *stands on a hillock dominating the skyline below the Chiltern escarpment. The church dates from the 15th century and was heavily restored by the Victorians, who added the embattled tower. Inside the church (which is normally locked), is a tablet to Sir John Russell, great grandson of Oliver Cromwell. Due to its close location to "Chequers", the church has welcomed several Prime Ministers as well as world statesmen. If you happen to see a rector, take a closer look. It could be the ghost of the Reverend Robert Wallace who was rector of the church before the Civil War. The reverend is said to regularly haunt the church and even the present rector has claimed to have seen his ghost.*

Returning to our route, take the track mentioned earlier, passing between the church car park and a beautiful cottage, and follow it until you see some wooden rails on the left, where there is a public footpath sign hidden in the hedge along with a yellow footpath arrow. Pass between the rails and follow a narrow path the other side, which runs along the left hand perimeter of a field. When the field perimeter bears left, leave it continuing straight on across the centre of the field. Ahead to your left now and clearly visible is the distinctive monument at the top of Coombe Hill, our next destination!

At the far side of the field pass between some wooden railings to arrive at a road. Turn right along the road and after approximately twenty metres, cross the road and join a signposted public bridleway the other side. The bridleway, at first, follows a gravel drive passing between "Coombe Farm" and "Coombe Hill Farm Cottage". After this, it passes to the right of Ellesborough golf club, at which point the gravel drive ends and the bridleway continues as a path. A short distance on, the path forks and you should take the left hand fork passing through a small gate to meet a crossing path.

Go straight over the crossing path and take the footpath opposite which leads up the side of Coombe Hill, marked at this point by a National Trust sign. The way up the side of the hill is very steep and will certainly test your fitness! It is probably at this point you will be howling for my blood. As you near the top, the path breaks free of the tree line and here you should take a narrow path left which runs diagonally up the grass slope of the hill. There are magnificent views to your left now across to Pulpit and Beacon Hills, Ellesborough church and the field through which you have just passed. Coombe Hill with its natural chalk grassland, is also worth stopping to enjoy. In summer it is covered with pretty chalkland flowers and visiting butterflies.

The path continues along the edge of the hill and you should follow it, ignoring all turnings off, and when in view, head for the gold flame capped monument at the top of the hill. On reaching the monument you will also meet the Ridgeway once more.

i

Coombe Hill, 852ft/257m (OS. 849067 Map 165) *is not as many people believe, the highest point in the Chilterns, but the highest open hill. The highest point is actually at Wendover Woods to the north. The views from the hill are magnificent and on a clear day you can even see the Cotswold hills fiftyfive miles away. Some say it is also possible to see the Welsh mountains, though I find this hard to believe. The magnificent stone monument at the top of the hill is a landmark for miles around. It was erected in 1904 to commemorate the men of Buckinghamshire who lost their lives fighting the Boer War. The monument was almost destroyed in 1938 when it was hit by lightening.*

In front of the Boer monument is a direction finder enabling you to identify the views. Coombe Hill is the highest point on the Hampden Howler which I am sure you will learn with some cheer!

Our route, leaving the monument, can be a little confusing so great attention must be given to the instructions. From the monument, continue along the edge of the hill (do not go back on yourself but follow the scarp slope), following the higher path and not the Ridgeway. This may be difficult to discern as, at the time of writing, the Ridgeway marker looks as though it is indicating the higher path. The path continues above the Ridgeway through an area of open grass intersperced with gorse. The Ridgeway, to your left, now begins its slow descent of Coombe Hill to Wendover (you should not be descending). Gradually, the path you are on bends right and forks (take care not to miss this - if you find yourself bending sharp right again and following a fence with enclosed woodland on your left, then you will have gone too far and should retrace your steps to find the fork), where you should take the left hand fork, going over a crossing path, to follow a fence on your right enclosing woodland.

After a short distance, you will arrive at a pair of kissing gates. Pass through the left hand kissing gate to enter an area of beautiful ancient woodland called The Scrubs and go over a crossing track, a bridleway marked by blue arrows, immediately after which you will meet two paths leading through the wood ahead. Take the right hand path, marked by a yellow arrow on a tree trunk, just after which you will pass a National Trust sign stating "Footpath Only, No Horses. Motorcycles Prohibited".

Follow the path ahead through perhaps the most attractive beech woodland traversed so far and keep to the yellow direction arrows on the tree trunks. After a short distance, you will meet a wider path coming in from the left and here you should bear right to follow this, running parallel with a bank and a line of beech trees on the left.

After a short distance, look out for a yellow arrow on one of the beech trees mentioned (take care not to miss it), and on finding it, bear left to pass through the line of beech trees, also passing between some old iron fencing. After this, follow a prominent path leading in a straight line through the wood and away from the bank, with your route still marked by the now familiar yellow arrows. At points along the way you will pass the remains of old iron fencing which were once part of an estate here. The path is also level now, a pleasant change to the undulating hillside of the past few miles. The path later meets the corner of a field on the left and at the same time, the tree lined bank rejoins from the right. To clarify, you should now be walking between a fence on your left and the tree lined bank on your right. There is also a track running parallel with the path on the right. Further on you should ignore a marked footpath (yellow arrow) off to the right and carry straight on.

Eventually, the path passes through some wooden railings to meet a wide track with a cattle grid on your left. Ignore the track and carry straight on along a now fenced path, marked as a bridleway (blue arrow), still following the old iron fencing. A short distance on you will meet a crossing path, the left route being a bridleway and the right a public footpath. Ignore both of these and continue ahead, still following the iron fencing.

As the wood thins out and the iron fencing on your left ends, you should ignore another signposted footpath on the left, continuing ahead to eventually reach a stile beside a wooden rail. Cross the stile to arrive at a crossing track, a bridleway, onto which you should turn right. The track almost immediately bends left to run beside a garden on your left, marking the outskirts of Dunsmore village. Ignore all turnings off and keep to the bridleway to shortly join a semi-tarmacked lane which, in turn, you should follow ahead through the centre of Dunsmore. You will soon meet "The Fox Inn", a free house.

After "The Fox Inn", continue to follow the lane to eventually arrive at a crossroads in front of the village pond. The track ahead and not part of our route, once led to another pub, "The Black Horse", but this like so many other Chiltern pubs, has recently become a private residence. Turn right at the crossroads in the direction of the sign for Kimble and Princes Risborough and after approximately thirty metres, look out for a signposted footpath on your left. Take this going over a stile beside a gate to do so and follow a prominent path diagonally right across a field.

A few paces into the field, leave the main path which runs steeply down into a valley, to bear left instead heading for a stile and fence at the far side. This path is not well used so take care to ensure you do not take the wrong path (if you find yourself at the bottom of the valley you will have to retrace your steps to join the correct route). Go over the stile at the far side of the field and proceed diagonally right across the centre of the next field, heading for another stile the other side.

Go over the stile and continue diagonally right across the centre of a third field. You now have a lovely view of "Dunsmore Old Farm" nestling in the valley below. Go over a stile near the far right hand corner of the field and continue ahead along a fairly prominent path across a smaller field to reach and cross a stile at the far left hand corner. After the stile, go down a bank to meet a marked bridleway. Turn left along the bridleway which runs along the bottom of the valley and follows the line of some fields on your right.

When the fields end the bridleway forks and you should take the right hand fork, a few paces on ignoring a footpath (white arrow) off to the left. The fork you have taken, a bridleway, now enters more Chiltern woodland, Hampdenleaf Wood, and begins to climb gently uphill. A short time later, a track joins from the left which you should follow ahead, still going uphill, later ignoring a track on the right. Soon after this, your track bends sharp left and levels out to run through a more open part of Hampdenleaf Wood.

You should stay on the track, ignoring all minor turnings off, to eventually arrive at the remote hamlet of Little Hampden in front of "The Rising Sun Inn", free house. The pub which has recently been extended, has an upmarket image and muddy boots must be left outside.

Facing the pub, turn left along the lane and after approximately twenty metres, turn right along a concrete drive signposted as a public footpath. This leads past two pretty cottages and on meeting the second cottage, do not enter the garden but take a narrow hedged path ahead. Follow this to soon arrive at a field, where you should go over a crossing track and then straight across the centre of the field.

At the far side of the field, continue to follow the path through a strip of woodland and at the other side, on entering another field, bear diagonally right across the field heading for a gap in the wood below to your right. At this point, there are good views ahead across a sweeping valley known as Hampden Bottom. At the far side, immediately after entering the woodland, you will meet a crossing path onto which you should turn left. This soon bends right to follow a narrow strip of woodland down the side of the valley to eventually meet a lane **(OS. 847035).**

Go over a stile beside a gate to reach and cross the lane and at the other side, go over another stile into a field. Cross the field in the direction of a footpath sign, following a prominent path and heading for the tree line the other side. If the field has just been ploughed, you should make for a point roughly a third of the way in from the right (there are also white posts placed across the field to guide you). The scenery here is particularly beautiful and very different to that passed so far, to your left the valley sweeps round in a gradual curve with, to your near left nestling neatly at the valley bottom, "Hampden Bottom Farm".

At the far side of the field go over a stile beside a wooden gate and follow a narrow path ahead. At first however, you may want to stop for a breather and take time to admire the views back. The path runs gently uphill through woodland, at one point passing a giant redwood tree, a rarity and an indication that this was once estate land, part of "Hampden House". Eventually, the path leads to a stile which you should cross, thereby leaving the wood, to enter a field. Go straight ahead across the field passing to the right of the gothic style "Hampden House".

Hampden House (OS. 848025 Map 165), *from Norman times up until recently, was the seat of the powerful Hampden family, Earls of Buckingham. The Hampden estate was given to the family by Edward the Confessor in the 11th century. The current*

i

house, built on the site of the original house, is believed to date from the 14th century and was altered in the 18th century to its current appearance. The Hampden family were for centuries one of the most powerful families in England, but undoubtedly the most famous of the Hampden's was John Hampden, the Parliamentarian, 1594-1643. He was cousin and close friend of Oliver Cromwell and together, in their early years, they attempted to emigrate to America to avoid taxes. They were prevented in doing so when their ship was seized. History would have been very different had they succeeded.

John Hampden, being a Parliamentarian, came into constant conflict with the King, Charles I. This culminated in his arrest, along with four other Knights, for refusing to pay a new tax disguised as a loan by the King. He was arrested at "Hampden House" in a room called "The Brick Parlour" which still exists today. His imprisonment was short-lived and Hampden continued to oppose the King, who dissolved one Parliament after another. During this time Hampden was instrumental in the death of two of Charles' most loyal aids, the Duke of Buckingham who was murdered by a friend of Hampden's and the Earl of Strafford who was beheaded following what some believe to have been trumped up charges.

John Hampden really shot to fame in 1636 when he refused to pay another new tax known as the Ship Tax. Hampden declared the tax illegal for it had not been approved by a Parliament which the King had already dissolved. A famous story tells of John Hampden riding into Great Kimble church during a service and encouraging the church-goers to follow him to London in a protest against the tax. In 1637, he was prosecuted before the Court of the Exchequer for not paying the tax. He lost his case but only by seven votes to five, which was seen as a victory by his supporters as the jurors had been under threat from the King. Hampden immediately found himself the most popular man in the country and an arch enemy of the King.

In 1642, after a period when Parliament had had the upper hand, the King again tried to arrest Hampden along with five of his colleagues at the House of Commons. Hampden had received advanced warning of this and together with his colleagues, escaped to declare open war against the King. Charles panicked and sent his wife packing with some of the Crown jewels to the Continent, whilst he prepared for Civil War at York. The Civil War was to bring Hampden's death. After displaying great bravery at the first battle of the war, the Battle of Edgehill, Hampden was mortally wounded in trying to prevent Prince Rupert, "The Mad Cavalier", from returning to Oxford after his men had ransacked Chinnor. Hampden was carried from the battle ground at Chalgrove and taken to Thame where he was to die. His last words were, "Receive my soul, O Lord. Save my country; O Lord be merciful to ....". He thus passed away unable to complete his final prayer.

Hampden died a hero and was carried back to "Hampden House" by his men and later buried at the church. In the 19th century, the grave was opened by Lord Nugent who was writing Hampden's biography and wanted to confirm how he had died. The body was said to be in such perfect condition that he was immediately recognised from a portrait hanging in the house.

Over the years the house has seen many important visitors, both friend and foe. Queen Elizabeth I is known to have stayed at Hampden and there is an interesting story regarding the visit of King Edward III and his son, the Black Prince. Whilst staying, the Black Prince is said to have received a punch on the nose from his host during a quarrel. The Prince and his father reputedly left in a rage and later confiscated estates belonging to the Hampden's. This led to the following, badly written, rhyme.

> *"Tring, Wing and Ivinghoe,*
> *Hampden did forgoe,*
> *For striking of a blow,*
> *And glad he did 'scape so"*

The last of the Hampden's died in 1985. During the second World War, the house was turned into a girls school and more recently, a film studio. Watch closely for the next recently made horror film on television. You will probably recognise "Hampden House".

At the far side of the field, go over a stile beside a gate to reach a track. Turn left along the track and after a few paces, pass through a small wooden gate to pass beside the old stables which have been converted into conference rooms. The track which forms part of the drive way to the house, follows the line of the ancient earthwork, Grims Ditch. It originally ran along the top of the bank but this was levelled for the visit of Elizabeth I to afford the Queen an easier approach.

Continue ahead to reach the church and take a path right which leads through the churchyard, passing to the right of the church. Follow this round to the other side of the church where you will arrive at the entrance.

i
†
Hampden Church (OS. 848024 Map 165) *is of Norman origin, dating from when the first house was built, though none of the original architecture can be seen today. The earliest visible remains are the 13th century nave and main door. Inside, stands the font which has baptised the Hampden's since they arrived in England together with a number of interesting memorials, including a particularly unusual one to John Hampden. Unfortunately, due to mindless vandals, the church has to be kept locked to protect them.*

With your back to the church door, follow the path ahead to leave the churchyard via a kissing gate into a field. Continue ahead along the right hand perimeter of the field to, after a short distance, pass through another kissing gate and continue through a rough fenced area which protects a pond. It is worth pausing here to look back at the church. At the other side of the fenced pond, go through another kissing gate and carry straight on, again along the right hand perimeter of the field. At the far side, pass through yet another kissing gate and continue ahead through a strip of woodland to reach a tarmac drive. In the trees on your left you will see an ancient burial mound.

Go over the drive and continue along a narrow path ahead which acts as a dividing line between two fields. Ahead to your left now are the rooftops of Great Hampden, our next destination. At the end of the fields, ignore a signposted footpath left and carry straight on along a now fenced path which runs between a field on your left and a small copse on your right. This soon follows the line of a hedge to a house on the left and shortly arrives at a kissing gate beside a pair of gates. Pass through the kissing gate to meet a lane.

Turn left along the lane and follow it to shortly arrive at a crossroads and "The Hampden Arms" pub, a free house serving a good selection of real ales and an excellent range of food. Go straight across the road and follow another road ahead, signposted to Bryants Bottom and High Wycombe. A few paces on, turn right onto a signposted public footpath beside a bus stop. The footpath runs along the right hand perimeter of the village cricket green where there are a number of conveniently placed benches on which you can rest and enjoy a game. The cricket green was laid in 1950, mainly due to the efforts of the last Earl of Buckingham.

At the far side of the cricket green, follow the path ahead to go over a stile and enter Hampden Common, predominantly woodland. Follow a prominent path ahead along the edge of the common, ignoring all turnings off and taking head of the white arrows marked on tree trunks. You should later ignore a marked footpath off to the left and pass a large hollow on your right before arriving at a gate and stile in front of a lane.

Go over the stile and turn right along the lane where after a few paces, you will arrive at a crossroads. Take a signposted bridleway ahead to your left here, the other side of the road, signposted to Speen. To do this, pass between two wooden posts and then some thin wooden railings, after which you should bend left to follow a quite prominent path, also marked with white arrows and the painted word "footpath". The path leads through the south eastern edge of Monkton Wood where you should ignore all turnings off, keeping to the main path and following the white arrows on the tree trunks.

After approximately half a mile, the path arrives at a junction of paths near the far side of the wood. Here, you should pass through another set of wooden rails (these are frail and could easily disappear in the future), after which you should turn right onto a crossing path which runs along the edge of the wood with fields on your left. Keep to the path along the edge of the wood, later passing a house on the left, before eventually passing through another set of wooden rails to arrive beside a cottage on your left **(OS. 831015)**. Follow the path round in front of the cottage, ignoring a marked path on the right, to arrive at Lily Bottom Lane where you should turn right.

Follow the lane to its end, a "T" junction, beside "The Lily and Pink" pub, a free house at the hamlet of Parslows Hillock. *The pub which has been extensively modernised to create a plush interior, has a story to tell. It is named after a Mr. Pink, a butler and Miss Lily, a maid. They both worked at "Hampden House" until they married and moved here to run the pub. The pub also has a literary connection, for it was a regular haunt of the first World War poet, Rupert Brooke. Like many poets his work became most popular after his death. He died whilst on active service at the tender age of nineteen. Displayed inside are a few lines penned by the poet in praise of "The Pink and Lily". No doubt the pub is also among the "inn fires" Brooke mentions in one of his most moving poems, "The Chilterns".*

From the lane beside "The Pink and Lily", turn right along a road in the direction of a sign for Hampden and Missenden and after approximately twenty metres, leave it as it bends right to join a track on the left, marked as a public bridleway. Follow this for a few metres before turning right, still following the bridleway signs, passing through a wooden gate to thereafter follow a track ahead through Hillock Wood. Keep to the track until you arrive at a crossing path (take care not to miss it), marked by white arrows. Turn left here to follow the path downhill which in places has steps to assist your progress and to prevent you from descending too quickly!

Eventually, the path arrives at a stile which you should cross to leave the wood and continue ahead along the right hand perimeter of a field. This near final stretch is a lovely way to finish the walk, with the wooded hills, rolling fields and vale stretched out before you, encompassing an idyllic Chiltern scene. At the far side of the field, go over a stile and maintain your route ahead across the centre of the next field, heading for the lovely flint "Brimmers Farm". At the far side of this field, go over a stile and turn right, along a lane in front of the farm.

Follow the lane until you see a drive on your left with an entrance of brick pillars and signposted as a public bridleway and circular walk. Take this and later, as the drive bends left, leave it by going over a stile on your right to thereafter follow a prominent path across the centre of a field, running along the bottom of a shallow valley. At the far side of the field, turn right along the field perimeter to immediately pass a pretty pond formed from a spring and protected by horse chestnut trees. As you continue you are encouraged by the welcoming sight of the Whiteleaf Cross, an indication that you do not have far to go.

At the corner of the field go over a stile onto a track, our friend the Upper Icknield Way and Ridgeway path. Turn right along the track passing behind a school and thereafter some houses, before arriving at a road, New Road. Turn left along the road retracing your steps to the roundabout, our starting point. If you have the energy you can now explore the town!

Princes Risborough (OS. 807035 Map 165) *has a pretty main street from which a lane bordered by timber framed cottages leads to the town's Norman church. Beside the church are some earthworks known as The Mount, believed to have once been a Saxon camp. The church itself has been much altered over the centuries, but still gives the impression of being old. Behind the church is the old manor house and a small pond, all that remains of the moat. Buckinghamshire has more moated houses than any other county in England, probably because of its position and, in the past, more than its fair share of powerful families.*

ACCOMMODATION

The Red Lion, Whiteleaf. Tel: 0844 344476
Approximately a quarter of a mile from the walk, accommodation is in one of four en suite bedrooms in a cosy traditional pub.

Youth Hostel, Bradenham YHA, Bradenham. Tel: 0494 56 2929
Approximately five miles from the walk, the hostel is in a converted Victorian school at the edge of the village green. It is only a few minutes walk to the village pub, "The Red Lion", making this an ideal place to stay if you are on a budget.

Camping and Caravanning, Karma Farm, Radnage. Tel: 0494 484136
Approximately seven miles from the walk, this is a Camping and Caravanning Club certified site for members only. (To join, tel. 0203 694886). It is in a beautiful location with fine views and good facilities.

THE CHRISTMAS CRACKER

Distance: 13½ miles (21.75 km)

Time: Allow approximately 7 hours

Map: Ordnance Survey Landranger Map 175

START
FINGEST
80M

IBSTONE
COMMON
212M

CHRISTMAS
COMMON
240M

FINISH
FINGEST
80M

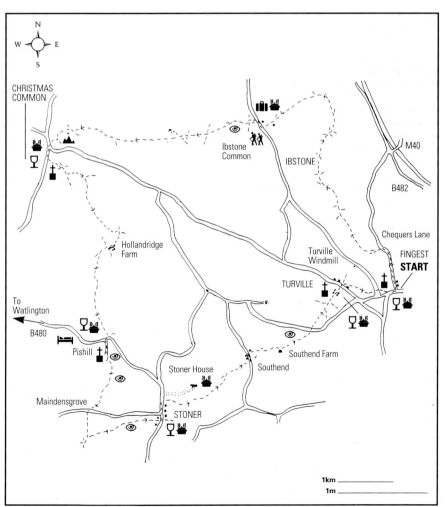

77

Walk Summary

This is a glorious walk taking you through some of the most unspoilt countryside and prettiest villages the Chilterns have to offer. The route is undulating passing in and out of wooded valleys and over hills where you are occasionally rewarded with some truly superb views, especially on the last third of the walk. Along the way, you will discover some excellent hostelries placed at convenient intervals to allow regular breaks. Above all, do not rush this walk and you will have a day to remember for months to come.

Start - OS. 777911 Map 175

The walk starts from in front of "The Chequers" pub at Fingest. From the north Fingest is best reached via the B482 from Stockenchurch. Shortly after passing over the M40 you will see a lane south, signposted to Fingest. From the south, it is best from the A4155 at Mill End, to join the Hamble Valley road and follow this through Skirmett from where Fingest is signposted. An alternative start can be made from Ibstone Common (OS. 751939), which is easily reached from junction 5 of the M40. The nearest railway station is at Henley.

THE CHRISTMAS CRACKER

The walk starts from Fingest, a pretty village in an idyllic Chiltern setting.

Fingest (OS. 777911 Map 175) is dominated by its church which has an unusually large tower, topped by a double gabled saddleback roof. Built by the Normans, save for the roof added in the 18th century, the church has remained virtually unaltered to the present day. The tower which rises sixty feet and has walls which are four feet thick, is so different from the slender nave, that it appears to have originally been part of another church. In fact, the church as we see it today is as the Normans built it. Perhaps after the expense of the tower, their plans for the nave were forced to be somewhat more moderate.

North of the church, once stood a palace built for the Bishops of Lincoln. It is rumoured that tunnels led from the palace to the church but if this is true, they still remain undiscovered. There are also stories of ghostly ladies haunting the churchyard at night and of one of the bishops, Henry Burgwash, who is said to roam the local countryside dressed as a forester. The latter is believed to have confiscated local common land from the villagers and, it is said, is now paying for his sin by having to protect the land for eternity.

Opposite the church stands the 17th century "Chequers" pub, Brakspear's, which has retained many of its original features. The bars are cosy with some ornately carved seats, low beamed ceilings and open fires. A wide range of bar food is available and the pub also has a separate restaurant. There is a large garden at the rear. The name "Chequers" probably refers to our earliest bankers and money lenders. Before purpose built banks became part of our High Streets, financial transactions were usually conducted at selected pubs. These transactions were normally done over a chequered board and when business was in progress at a pub, a chequered board would be displayed outside. This is the reason why so many of our pubs have the name "Chequers". It is also the reason why current day money orders are called cheques.

From the pub take the lane opposite marked as Chequers Lane, passing to the right of St. Bartholemew's church and to the left of some very pretty cottages converted from an old barn. Keep to the lane which leaves the village following the bottom of a lovely valley. A short distance on, you will pass the picturesque "Manor Farm" (note the large clock face on one of the barns) and after this, you should ignore a signposted footpath on the right, to continue along the lane for approximately thirty metres where the lane bends right. Here, you should leave it to join a signposted bridleway on the left.

Almost immediately after joining, ignore a couple of footpaths off to the left (the second going over a stile beside a metal gate) and keep to the bridleway which bears right to run through a narrow strip of woodland between fields. After a short distance, you will arrive at a gate through which you should pass to follow a fenced path between fields. There are lovely views here to your left and right to Turville Hill and Hanger Hill respectively. The upper wooded slopes of the hills are a favourite haunt of deer, so keep your eyes peeled as they often descend to the fields around you to graze. After a short distance, the bridleway passes beside a now obsolete wooden gate and you should continue ahead through another strip of woodland.

After some distance, the bridleway meets a track onto which you should turn right to continue through the strip of woodland. A few paces on, ignore another track off to the right and soon after, a footpath left marked by a white arrow on a gatepost, to continue ahead along the valley bottom to shortly meet and cross a stile beside a gate. At the other side, ignore a crossing track and carry straight on, initially through an old hazel coppice which gradually gives way to pine.

Later, ignore a marked bridleway (blue arrow) on your left to soon after arrive at a crossing track where, as a guide, there are a pair of metal gates and a farm building on your right. Go over the crossing track and join a track the other side, slightly to your right, marked by a white arrow. This runs through Penley Wood, again a mixture of hazel and pine. After some distance, you will arrive at a grass clearing and crossing track with gates on either side. Ignore the crossing track to maintain your route ahead through Penley Wood, keeping to the main track and ignoring all further turnings off including, sometime later, one marked by white arrows. Soon after the latter, the track you are on in turn becomes well marked by white arrows and you should keep to it for roughly another three quarters of a mile, where you must look out for a pair of arrows painted on a tree on the left, with one of the arrows forking off the main route **(OS. 761944)**. Beneath this is written "20 yards ahead".

Leave the main track here to take the left fork and join a narrow grass track which runs along the perimeter of Penley Wood. Shortly after, you will arrive at a field where you should continue ahead along the left hand perimeter. At the far side of the field, go over a crossing track to join a path ahead which leads through Hartmoor Wood. The easy walking of the last few miles now changes as the path begins a long slow ascent out of the valley to Ibstone Common.

The climb becomes steeper as you progress and the path eventually comes out at the far side of the wood where it joins a track at the edge of a field. Carry straight on, following the left hand perimeter of the field, to soon join a track coming from "Chilsley Farm" on your left, marked on the Ordnance Survey map as "Chilsley Grange". Follow the farm track making for the houses of Ibstone visible ahead and stay on the track as it leaves the field, passing between houses to eventually arrive at a lane in front of Ibstone Common.

Ibstone (OS. 752938 Map 175) *is a scattered village straddling a long ridge. The church at the far end of the village is worth visiting after the walk. It dates from the 12th century and has some interesting carvings above the door from that period. The* *village has moved since the building of the church which now stands isolated. In later centuries an attempt was made to build another church nearer the new village centre and not far from the point at which you are standing. For some reason, it kept collapsing and local superstition blamed the devil. The site is consequently now known as Hell Corner.*

Cross the lane and turn right to follow it looking out for "Yew Tree Cottage" on your right with its two shapely yew trees from which it takes its name. After a short distance, you will meet a signposted public bridleway on the left which you should take. At first however, you may wish to continue for a few paces more along the lane, to enjoy your first refreshment stop in the form of "The Fox". This is a small country hotel which has a bar open to non-residents.

Take the bridleway mentioned (in summer this can become overgrown with bracken despite being regularly cleared), and follow it going over a narrow crossing path to, after a few winding metres (approximately twenty metres), arrive at a much more prominent crossing path onto which you should turn left. Keep to the path, ignoring all minor turnings off, to shortly pass a murky pond on your right, soon after which you will arrive at a wide track marked by a white arrow.

Turn right along the track which runs between a couple of narrow fields before forking in front of a sign for the Wormsley Estate. Pass to the left of the sign and follow a marked bridleway (white arrow) downhill, ignoring another path off to the left sometime later. You will now descend through a newly planted area of woodland, established to replace trees destroyed by the infamous storm of 1987. As you descend, the bridleway runs between banks before entering an area of the wood which escaped the storm.

Soon after entering this mature woodland, look out for a marked footpath (white arrow - "S21") on the left which you should take. Take care not to miss it. The footpath immediately takes you steeply down the side of the hill and suddenly breaks out from the wood to arrive at an open field. You are straight away rewarded with lovely views across a wide valley at the centre of which lies Hale Wood. This area in summer is a mass of wild flowers and makes for a pleasant place to stop for a rest and maybe an early picnic.

The footpath bends right to follow the perimeter of the field and continues gently downhill. In summer it is lined by yet more wild flowers visited by a mass of butterflies. On reaching the corner of the field and the bottom of a valley, go over a stile and across a crossing track, to go over another stile the other side beside a Wormsley Estate sign. This takes you into another field where you should continue ahead straight across the field. As you progress, if you look to your right, you will see the tall Stockenchurch telecommunications tower, somewhat out of place in this very rural scene.

At the far side of the field, go over a stile and cross a tarmac lane and thereafter, cross another stile into yet another field. Go diagonally left across the field heading for a gate at the far left hand corner and on reaching it, cross a stile beside the gate to thereafter, turn right along a wide track. After approximately fifty paces, turn left leaving the track to join a footpath marked by a white arrow on an electricity pole. The footpath initially follows a brick and flint wall on the right, after which it continues through an avenue of trees. As you progress, you should ignore another path off to the left marked as footpath "SH8".

The footpath you are following now runs through woodland and your way is guided by white arrows painted on tree trunks. Go over a crossing track and continue ahead passing to the left of a stone urn (this has only just been placed here and could just as quickly disappear in the future), to meet another track where you should turn left, still following the white arrows. The track winds through an area of open and newly planted woodland and continues for a short distance before forking. Take the left hand fork, thereby leaving the track and continue along a path through a short stretch of beech wood. Thereafter, you will start to climb gently uphill through Blackmoor Wood.

Some distance on, ignore a path leading off to the left marked by a white arrow on a tree and "SH6", to carry straight on. After this, the path levels out for a while, running along the side of the hill. This part of the wood is extremely attractive with numerous glades, lush with woodland grasses and wild flowers and home to an abundance of wildlife. Sometime on, the path starts to climb once more to head for Christmas Common, where, to give you an incentive, there is one of the best pubs on the walk, if not in the Chilterns.

As you climb towards Christmas Common the path enters an area of more mature woodland, Shotridge Wood, dominated by stately and well established beech trees. Ignore a crossing track sometime later and carry straight on, still following the white arrows, to eventually meet the edge of the wood where there is a field visible ahead. Another path marked "SH5" joins from the left at this point. You should ignore this and continue to follow the original path which now bends right and after a few paces, turn left onto another path this time unmarked. As a guide, this is just as the field on the left ends.

Follow the path which runs in a straight line through the wood, now mainly oak, to shortly arrive at another path onto which you should turn left. You are reassured that your directions are correct here, as the path is once again marked by the familiar white arrows which have been so prevalent throughout our walk. After a short distance the path forks. You can take either fork as they meet up again very soon, albeit immediately after, they fork once more. This time, you must take the left hand fork which follows the line of a field on your left, before leading out to a grass track. Follow the track which, after passing to the right of "Magpie Cottage", runs between fields and the two aerial masts which identify Christmas Common for miles around, to eventually arrive at a junction of two lanes.

Do not take the lane immediately to your left signposted to Northend and Turville, but take the second lane left signposted to Nettlebed and Henley. You will shortly arrive at the promised watering hole, "The Fox and Hounds", a Brakspear's pub and an excellent welcome to Christmas Common.

Christmas Common (OS. 714932 Map 175) *is a small hamlet originating from a small group of subsistence farms which used the common to graze animals. The common once stretched for several miles but was greatly reduced in 1272 by the Earl of Cornwall to create a deer park. The remainder of the common was enclosed during the 19th century.*

Apart from the pub, there is not a great deal to see, with probably the most interesting feature of the hamlet being its name. The origin is unclear. One story is that the hamlet gained its name during the Civil War when the opposing armies agreed a truce for the Christmas of 1643. Another theory and in my opinion the most likely, is that the common once acted as a communal gathering place to celebrate Christmas. Centuries ago, people living on the common would have been mainly travellers and the open common with its abundance of wood and holly nearby, would have been the ideal gathering place for Christmas celebrations.

Being rural folk, Christmas celebrations were probably based around the ancient fertility cermonies which rejoiced the passing of the shortest day and welcomed the far off season of spring. These ceremonies would probably have involved the burning of a holly bush which would have been carried aloft around the common. This was known as the mid-winter fire festival and was primarily to encourage the re-birth of the weakening sun. On Christmas Eve a large log would be set alight and left to burn for twelve days. This of course, is the yule log. The ashes were later scattered over the fields to ensure fertility. It is believed the twelve days represented the twelve months of the year. Yule is an ancient word for the month of December. Both traditions above, were brought to England by the Danes who also at time of the mid-winter festival, decorated their homes with greenery. In the 4th century the church adopted the mid-winter festival as the date to celebrate the birth of Christ.

You can celebrate another great event, the ancient tradition of raising your glass, for reaching the highest point on the walk!

To continue, follow the lane past the pub and after a short distance take a signposted footpath on the left, also marked as the Oxfordshire Way. This is just before the village chapel. Go over a crossing track and continue ahead along the footpath which runs through a young beech wood. Just before the wood ends the footpath forks and you should take the left hand fork, carrying straight on, to shortly arrive at a driveway in front of a flint and brick cottage.

Turn left here and after a few paces, join a semi-tarmacked lane. Do not take the signposted footpath the other side of the lane, but turn right along the lane itself to pass two picturesque cottages and, on your left, a small Christmas tree plantation. Continue until you reach a Forestry Commission sign for Queen and College Woods, where you should leave the tarmac lane to join a signposted bridleway on your left, also marked as the Oxfordshire Way. You will now walk through Queen Wood going downhill along a prominent track which sometime later, bends right before forking.

Take the right hand fork to follow the track along the bottom of a valley, again through typical Chiltern beech wood. Ignore all turnings off, following the track and blue arrows, to eventually arrive at a parking area used by the Forestry Commission for logging. Carry straight on through the parking area, ignoring tracks off to the left and right, thereby maintaining your route along the valley bottom. Continue for approximately another half a mile to reach a wide track off to the left and a narrow path off to the right, marked by white crossed arrows and a yellow arrow on a post.

Turn right here to follow the narrow footpath marked as "PS4" and "OW", the latter denoting that you are still following the Oxfordshire Way. Take care not to miss it. The footpath leads up the valley side to soon reach a stile which you should cross into a field, the open scenery here offering a pleasant change to the beech wood of the past few miles. Bear gently right to follow a prominent path uphill across the field in the direction of a yellow arrow and heading for a clump of trees the other side. As you near the top of the ridge, the farm buildings of "Hollandridge Farm" come into view. You should head just to the right of the farm buildings to reach and follow the left hand perimeter of the field ahead. To your left here are two small ponds, the first sometimes difficult to see in summer, but the second clearly visible. To your right, the two aerial masts at Christmas Common are also now in view.

At the far side of the field, go over a crossing track and then over a stile into another field, where you should continue ahead along the left hand perimeter. As the field perimeter bends left however, leave it and carry straight on heading for a stile ahead which is clearly visible. Cross the stile to enter College Wood (part of Greenfield Wood) and after a few paces when the footpath forks, take the left hand fork, the higher of the two paths. Sometime later, the path begins to descend and here gaps in the trees allow you to enjoy views across a valley which runs through the heart of the wood.

Soon after, the path levels out for a while to run along the side of the valley before descending once more. At the bottom of the valley, go over a stile to reach another footpath onto which you should turn left, thereby leaving the wood to enter a large open field. Follow the footpath, more a grass track, along the valley bottom where ahead of you in the distance, you can just see the top of the church at Pishill. This is another delightful part of the walk which allows you to appreciate the diversity of the Chiltern scenery.

At the far side the grass track leaves the field becoming fenced to shortly meet a road, the B480, beside the lovely "Pishill Farmhouse" on your left **(OS. 726901)**. Just before reaching the road, ignore a footpath which leads off to the left. Turn right along the road for a few paces and then left along a tarmac lane, once again signposted as the Oxfordshire Way and also "To Pishill Church". If however, you are a real ale addict and are in need of refreshment, then continue along the road a little further to arrive at "The Crown", a free house, at Pishill. You will have to retrace your steps to rejoin our walk.

"The Crown" *is a lovely thatched pub recently tastefully modernised, serving a good choice of real ales and some excellent food. It dates from the 11th century and has one of the largest priest holes in the country. This was hidden under the roof and was large enough to hide over twenty priests during the Reformation. A tragic story involving a priest has supposedly led to the pub being haunted. The story tells of the priest, Father Dominique, who whilst hiding at "The Crown", fell in love with a girl called Elizabeth who was staying at the pub. One night a nobleman also staying at "The Crown" became the worse for drink and clumsily attempted to seduce Elizabeth. When she refused his advances the man became angry and cursed loudly at her. Father Dominique hearing what was going on, quickly came down from his hiding place and in Elizabeth's defence, attacked the man with a sword displayed on the wall. Father Dominique being ill-acquainted with swords, was mortally wounded and later buried in Pishill churchyard. The ghost of the brave priest is said to appear wearing a black cloak and large hat. On occasions, loud knocking sounds are also to be heard coming from the roof.*

Returning to our route, follow the lane uphill passing between two cottages to soon arrive at Pishill church, unfortunately nearly always locked. *Despite its appearance the church was built in 1854 to replace an earlier Norman church. The name Pishill does not as the more uncouth version may suggest, describe where the locals relieved themselves. It means instead, "a hill where peas grow". In the 19th century, one poor chap, Wiggins, obviously misinterpreted the name and was prosecuted for "making a privey near the churchyard".*

Pishill Church

After the church, continue uphill, still following the lane, where you will gain increasingly good views left over Stonor Park. As the lane ends take a grass track ahead which follows the perimeter of a garden on your right. This is marked as bridleway "PS22" as well as the Oxfordshire Way. After a short distance the bridleway forks and you should take the left hand fork, still following the Oxfordshire Way. This almost immediately takes you into a field where you should continue ahead along the left hand perimeter, gradually descending into a valley.

Continue to the bottom of the valley and up the other side where the field soon ends. Here you should continue ahead, going over a crossing track, to follow a prominent path marked as a bridleway, uphill through woodland. The valley side is much steeper than the side descended and it can seem an age before you finally reach the top. When the path does eventually level out, it follows the line of a field on your right. Shortly after this, you should ignore a marked footpath off to the left (path "PS9"), maintaining your route ahead and still following the Oxfordshire Way ("OW").

The bridleway soon starts a leisurely descent and at a fork, you should keep left, in the direction of the Oxfordshire Way arrow, passing to the left of some houses which mark the edge of a scattered hamlet, Maidensgrove. The bridleway now descends quite steeply through a wood of beech and holly trees before arriving at a narrow lane **(OS. 723888)**. Cross the lane and join a marked bridleway the other side (ignore a track which forks left) and follow this uphill and along the edge of the wood, ignoring all further turnings off, until you reach the far side of the wood. Here, you should ignore a stile and footpath on your right to continue ahead, leaving the wood to enter a field.

Go straight across the field, making for the rooftops of a farm ahead of you. On nearing the far side, you will meet and should follow a track which runs along the right hand field perimeter. Pass under some electricity wires and just before reaching the field corner, turn left (thereby leaving the Oxfordshire Way) onto a marked footpath which takes you back across the centre of the field and under the electricity wires once more. As you cross the field there are marvellous views to your right of Bowsey and Ashley Hills in Berkshire and beyond to the North Hampshire Ridge.

At the far side of the field, go over a stile and follow a narrow footpath ahead through a beech wood. After a few paces, the footpath joins a track and you should carry straight on, in the direction of the white arrows, following the track downhill through the wood. Ignore all crossing tracks and any turnings off to the left or right, keeping to the main track and following the white arrows. At the far side of the wood, go over a stile to enter a field. This is a glorious spot and you are straight away rewarded with excellent views across the valley and immediately below, to Stonor, beyond which is "Stonor House". To your left and right are lovely views across the rest of the valley which, to your right, runs down to Henley on Thames and the Thames valley.

The path from here is undefined and you should simply carry straight on heading for the village of Stonor below. As you progress, a stile will come into view ahead just to the left of a circle of trees. Make for the stile and go over it to continue straight across the centre of the next field. At the far side, go over another stile and join a narrow fenced path ahead to soon meet the B480 at Stonor. Our route is left along the B480. However, if you have not taken advantage of the earlier refreshment stops, a short detour right (thirty metres) along the B480 will take you to "The Stonor Arms", an hotel and restaurant and a lovely place to stop (although muddy boots are discouraged). The menu is excellent allowing you to have as much or as little as you want. You will need to retrace your steps to rejoin our route.

Returning to our route, turn left along the B480 where shortly after, you should ignore a signposted public bridleway on the right and sometime on, a lane off to the left signposted to Maidensgrove and Russells Water. Continue instead until you see a footpath on your right signposted to Southend, 1½ miles. This is just before a forty miles per hour speed limit sign on the left hand side of the road. Take the footpath by passing through a kissing gate in a deer fence to enter Stonor Park. Follow the footpath ahead in the direction of the white arrows (your way is assisted and kept clear here, being regularly mowed by the park grounds people), climbing uphill.

On nearing the top there are good views left to "Stonor House". The path later levels out to follow the side of a valley and continues to afford good views left over the house and around you over the surrounding parkland. There are also lovely views behind to your left at this point to the valley at Pishill and the two aerial masts at Christmas Common, giving you some idea of the ground covered on your walk today - although I am sure your legs are beginning to tell you this anyway! After passing the house, you will arrive at a crossing track. Our route is straight on, but first I recommend a short detour left (when the house is open - April to September) along the track to visit the historic "Stonor House".

Stonor House (OS. 742893 Map 175) *is one of the great houses of our country and a monument to the Catholic faith. The house, although repeatedly modernised, dates essentially from the 13th century and from its conception has remained in the same family, the Stonor's (since 1838 Lord Camoys), to this day. The adjoining flint chapel is thought to have been built during the 14th century after a licence of mortmain was granted by King Edward III to build a place of worship.*

The Stonor family always were and still are staunch Catholics and over the centuries have been cruelly persecuted for their faith. Consequently, the house is riddled with secret passages and hiding places, even the small chapel conceals a priest hole. During the Reformation the Stonor's hid many priests in the house and no doubt sent some to "The Crown" for safe hiding. Such has been the Stonor's faith that the chapel is one of only three in the country to have continued uninterrupted worship during the Reformation.

The house has been home to a number of martyrs including Sir Adrian Fortescue, a cousin of Anne Boleyn beheaded at Tower Hill on 9th July, 1539, for refusing to recognise the King as the head of the Church. Stonor's most famous martyr however, was the Jesuit, Edmund Campion. Edmund, despite the risk of capture and death, continued to preach the Catholic faith wherever and whenever possible. At Stonor he helped set up a printing press in a secret room to print his controversial book, "Ten Reasons". The book was finished in time to be distributed at Oxford at the Comemoration. The authorities were furious and re-doubled their efforts to capture the Jesuit. Three weeks later, Edmund preached at Lyford near Wantage. Previously, such gatherings went unnoticed but following the publication of his book, huge crowds gathered to hear him and thence the authorities followed. He was arrested and taken on horseback to London wearing a hat inscribed, "Campion the Seditious Jesuit". At London he was tried and found guilty of conspiracy and was duly hanged. The following month a night raid under flaming torches was made on "Stonor House". Its occupants were arrested and the printing press seized. Edmund Campion was canonized in 1970, his feast day is 1st December.

Despite such violent persecution, the Stonor family remained loyal to their faith and after the Catholic Emancipation act of 1829, returned to public office. The house, still the home of the Stonor family, is fascinating to visit and an excellent guide book is available for sale detailing its eventful history. The old stables house a restaurant, another opportunity to stock up.

Returning to our route, go over the crossing track and continue ahead along the path ignoring any further crossing tracks. The terrain changes here from grass to open woodland, part of Balham's Wood. Sometime later, the footpath climbs to leave the valley which shelters "Stonor House" behind and leaves the park altogther by passing through a kissing gate in the deer fence. After the kissing gate, follow the path which runs through more dense woodland with a scattering of laurels at the base of the trees, to soon join a track which you should follow ahead. This climbs steadily and later meets another track. Join this to continue ahead, a few paces on ignoring another track off to the right. Soon after, you will arrive at a lane onto which you should turn left (ignoring a public footpath opposite), to walk through the hamlet of Southend.

i Follow the lane until you reach a concrete drive on your right, signposted as a public footpath. A house on your left, "Drovers", used to be a good pub but is now sadly closed. Turn right along the concrete drive mentioned and follow it, ignoring all turnings off, to its end at "Southend Farm". The drive passes to the left of the farm and as it bends right towards the farmhouse, leave it by going over a stile beside a metal gate ahead. Thereafter, continue straight on along the right hand perimeter of a field, where the views ahead now are of Turville Hill with its distinctive windmill and beyond, Hanger Wood.

Turville Windmill

As the perimeter of the field bends right, leave it to carry straight on along a grass track to reach the far side where you should cross a stile beside a metal gate. Thereafter, follow a wide fenced track ahead which runs downhill through woodland, part of Great Wood featured in "The Great Skirmett Skirmish". At the other side of the wood, go over a stile beside two metal gates and continue downhill, now following the left hand perimeter of a field. The windmill on Turville Hill is directly ahead. At the bottom of the field, cross over a stile and then a lane and go over another stile the other side. From here you should follow a prominent path across the centre of a field and on nearing the far side, ignore another path joining from the right.

At the end of the field, continue ahead through a gap in the hedge to join a fenced path which runs gently downhill between fields and eventually leads out to a small cul-de-sac. Carry straight on, passing an old school on your left and a number of pretty cottages, to arrive at Turville village green with the village church on your left.

Turville (OS. 768911 Map 175), *with footpaths converging on the village from every direction, is to the Chilterns what Edale is to the Peak District. Nearly every Chiltern walking book will carry a picture of Turville (this one included!) and no doubt here, you will meet many walkers, the majority converging on the pub. The village despite such attention, retains its dignity and undoubted beauty.*

entering Turville

Overlooking the village is Turville Hill with its Copstone windmill. There has been a mill on this site since the 13th century, though the current mill was built in the 17th century. It has been featured in several television productions but is most famous for its part in the film, "Chitty Chitty Bang Bang".

The village church dates from Norman times with some 14th century additions and a 15th century tower. Inside the church is a 13th century stone coffin which, when opened, not only contained the body of its intended, a priest, but also the body of a woman with a bullet hole in her skull. She was, following this, formally buried but as to who she was or indeed the identity of the perpetrator of her tragic end, remain a mystery.

The village pub, "The Bull and Butcher", Brakspear's, though often crowded, retains its rural and traditional atmosphere. Both bars are fairly small but cosy, with the main bar having a lovely open fire. There are normally fresh flowers on the tables and apart from the excellent Brakspear's ales, the pub offers an excellent menu. The pub's name is unusual, the bull is said to represent Anne Boleyn and the butcher, Henry VIII - no doubt derived from the area's Catholic connections. The origin of the pub itself is also interesting. During the early 17th century, masons who were working to restore the church went on strike until they received appropriate refreshment (beer). An enterprising local resident promptly applied for a licence and thus opened the pub.

To continue our walk, as you enter the village take the road to the right of the green and cross the road which runs through the centre of the village. At the other side, join a track signposted as a public footpath which passes between houses before forking at the base of Turville Hill. Take the right hand fork by going over a stile into a field, after which you should turn right to follow a footpath along the field perimeter, running behind a private garden. As the garden ends, follow a prominent path diagonally left across the field, going gently uphill, to reach and cross a stile at the far side. After this, follow a narrow footpath through an area of unkempt woodland and stay on it as it runs around the side of Turville Hill to eventually arrive at a lane.

Go over a stile and cross the lane and then a second stile the other side, to join a signposted public footpath. The footpath runs through more woodland and shortly meets a crossing path onto which you should turn right. The path joined, which is fenced, runs downhill between fields and sometime on, follows a brick and flint wall before arriving at the village of Fingest. Go over a stile to enter the village proper and follow the road ahead to reach our starting point, "The Chequers".

ACCOMMODATION

The Fox Country Hotel, Ibstone. Tel: 0491 638722
On the walk, this is a small comfortable hotel in the heart of the Chiltern countryside.

Bank Farm, Pishill. Tel: 0491 638601
Virtually on the walk, this is a lovely and relaxing place to stay. Accommodation is on a small working farm situated in a beautiful valley and opposite "The Crown" pub. What more could you want!

Youth Hostel, Bradenham YHA, Bradenham. Tel: 0494 562929
Approximately five miles from the walk, the hostel is in a converted Victorian school at the edge of the village green. It is only a few minutes walk to the village pub, "The Red Lion", making this an ideal place to stay if you are on a budget.

Camping and Caravanning, Gibbons Farm, Horsleys Green. Tel: 0494 482385
Approximately two miles from the walk, this is a small site in an area of outstanding natural beauty. It is open to Camping and Caravanning Club members only. For membership details, tel. 0203 694995.

THE HIGHMOOR HIKE

Distance: 13½ miles (21.75 km)

Time: Allow approximately 6½ hours

Map: Ordnance Survey Landranger Map 175

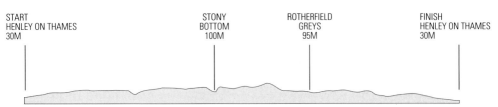

START	STONY	ROTHERFIELD	FINISH
HENLEY ON THAMES	BOTTOM	GREYS	HENLEY ON THAMES
30M	100M	95M	30M

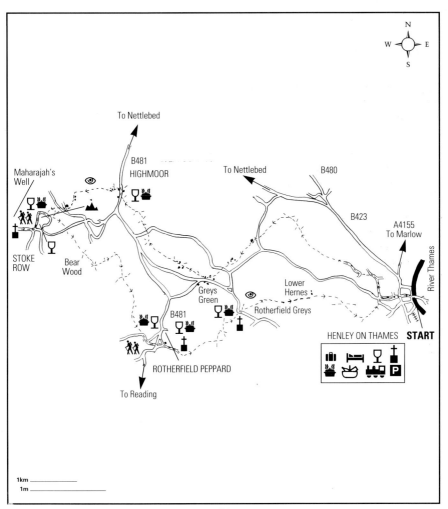

Walk Summary

This is a superb walk taking you through just about every type of scenery found in the Chilterns. In between open fields and enchanting woodland you will discover some timeless villages, some with pubs that stubbornly refuse to accept the 20th century. It is not an easy walk with many ups and downs and twists and turns, but on your return to Henley I can guarantee you will feel more than satisfied. One word of warning, some of the woodland paths can be very muddy, even in summer, so wear those boots!

Start - OS. 763826 Map 175

The walk starts from "The Angel" pub at Henley on the bridge over the river Thames. Getting to Henley is fairly straightforward as the town is served by several main roads. These are the A321, the A423 (at the time of writing being changed to the A4133) and the A4155. There are several car parks in Henley though probably the best and cheapest is Mill Meadows (signposted from the town centre), near the railway station. Unless you have local knowledge there are only two other viable alternative starts, Stoke Row (OS. 680840) and Rotherfield Peppard (OS. 708817), where there is a small car park on the common. For those travelling by train there is a station at Henley.

THE HIGHMOOR HIKE

The Angel on the Bridge

The walk starts from the famous "Angel" pub, Brakspear's, on Henley bridge. I say "on Henley bridge" as the pub which dates from the 14th century, incorporates one of the bridge's arches. This is because "The Angel" was one of several buildings, including a chapel, which were part of the original 14th century bridge. When the bridge was replaced in 1787 by the current structure, "The Angel" remained part of the bridge, just as it had been for centuries before.

There is much more to tell of Henley town though I prefer to leave this to the end of the walk, when you can enjoy learning the town's history over a well deserved drink in one of Henley's many hostelries. Instead, I think we should concentrate at this moment on Henley's and perhaps the Chilterns' most famous resident, Brakspear's brewery.

Brakspear's Brewery (OS. 762829 Map 175). *You will no doubt, whilst bravely* i
walking through the pages in this book, come to realise that I am somewhat of an
enthusiast of real ale and, in particular, the ales brewed by Brakspear. Part of every
adventure is discovering a new pub and, as virtually every walk encounters a
Brakspear's pub, it seems only fitting to learn something of this Henley brewery.

It is Robert Brakspear who we must principally thank for establishing the Brakspear
brewery we know today. Robert Brakspear was born in 1750 at Faringdon, near
Oxford. His father was a tailor by trade and from all accounts, the family was not
well off. The first family connection with brewing came in 1768, when Robert's uncle
became a partner in Henley's Bell Street Brewery. At that time Henley was a busy
market town specializing in corn and malt which was transported along the river on
huge barges to London. Having so much available malt and famous for its
abundance of fresh water, Henley had naturally turned to brewing and in the mid-
18th century, the town boasted two breweries as well as a large number of
independent hostelries brewing their own ale.

Robert personally became involved in brewing at the early age of nineteen when he
became landlord of "The Cross Keys" at Witney, a pub which still exists today. He
struck up a close relationship with his uncle and a few years later, was brewing and
selling his own beer to five other pubs in Witney. In 1779, Robert's uncle who was
now also his godfather, brought Robert to the Henley brewery and two years later
made him a partner.

Twenty one years later, Robert became the sole owner of the brewery and through his
skill and determination, steadily grew the business until in the year of his death in
1812. At that time, it controlled thirtyfour pubs and was producing on average, six
thousand, two hundred and fifty barrels of beer each year. Ironically, just before his
death and at the height of his success, Robert was faced with the possibility that the
brewery might be forced to close. The lease covering the brewery building and eight of
the pubs was due to expire in 1813 and to compound this problem, his eldest son
showed no interest in taking over the business. His only other son was, at that time,
just ten years old.

Only months from his death, Robert amalgamated the brewery with its closest rival
in New Street. Part of the complicated arrangement was that in 1825 the brewery
should admit his youngest son as a partner with a half share in the business. Thus,
when Robert died on 22nd November, 1812, he had ensured that the family interests
remained in the brewery.

After Robert's death the brewery moved to New Street where it continues to this day.
As was Robert's wish, his youngest son, William, entered as a partner in 1825 and
with good business acumen and a small amount of good fortune, took the brewery
from strength to strength. William became sole proprietor and in later years brought
both his sons into the business. On his death in 1882, the brewery had eighty pubs
and was producing fourteen thousand barrels of beer each year. This century the
brewery has continued under the management of the Brakspear family, though
sometimes through troubled times. Smaller breweries around Henley slowly closed
one by one, but Brakspear's despite competition from the new breed of national
brewers, continued to hold its own and even continued to grow. At its height the
brewery controlled over one hundred and fifty pubs.

As a traditional brewery, perhaps Brakspear's most important tradition is the hanging of the holly and mistletoe at Christmas. The holly branch is collected from Howe Hill and the mistletoe from Stonor. On Christmas morning they are hung by a large hook from a beam supporting the roof over the loading bay in the yard. Tradition has it that if they remain there all year, the company will continue to prosper. To date, the holly and mistletoe have never fallen, being religiously replaced every year.

Let us do our part for tradition by raising a glass of Brakspear's ale to the brewery and let's do it in as many of their pubs as possible!

Perhaps it is wise to keep tradition until a little later on when we have some miles under our belt. Therefore, from the pub, do not cross the bridge but walk up the High Street to immediately pass Henley church. At a crossroads controlled by traffic lights, carry straight on to immediately after cross the road on your right and turn left the other side to continue past the Town Hall, which also houses the Tourist Information centre. You will, at the same time, pass "The Kings Head" pub on your right, Brakspear's, which also offers B&B.

On meeting a second crossroads behind the Town Hall, carry straight on to follow West Street which has a number of fine cottages as well as an excellent small pub, "The Row Barge", Brakspear's, which also offers overnight accommodation. Follow West Street to its end, where you should turn right onto a narrow road signposted to Hop Gardens and public footpath to Fairmile. The lane leads past some lovely Victorian houses and cottages and nearing the end, past more modern houses designed to give the best views over Henley and the river, though unfortunately, they block your view as you walk! At a "T" junction, turn left and follow a road along the edge of a small housing estate and continue until the first row of houses on the left ends beside a turning area. Here you should turn left onto a signposted public footpath beside house number 71 **(OS. 754832)**. Take care not to miss it.

The footpath initially leads uphill between gardens and then turns right to run behind houses, still climbing. It eventually arrives at a narrow lane onto which you should turn right. As you progress, where gaps in the hedge allow, you will enjoy good views right across the Henley Fairmile, now the majestic route of the A423, to "Henley Park". Follow the lane passing a number of attractive properties, until it bends right into the last house, where you should leave it to cross a stile ahead onto a golf course. (There are a couple of gates along the lane. If these are shut simply cross the stile beside them).

Maintain your route ahead, now following a track which leads across the golf course. As one would expect in the Chilterns, the fairways here are lined with magnificent beech trees, a remnant of the woods which were once part of a medieval deer park. Keep to the track (do not turn off onto one of the paths leading to the greens), which gradually thins out and then bends left, where you should leave it to carry straight on in the direction of a footpath sign. Take head of the warning sign here also, "Beware of Golf Balls", especially if you want to complete this and any future walks!

As a guide, you should now be walking to the right of a row of scots pines and as these end you should continue ahead, gradually bearing right to leave the golf course by taking a prominent path ahead through Lanbridge Wood. Like most woodland paths this one diverges, forks and rejoins on a number of occasions, very much the result of years of bypassing muddy troughs. *In the years before tarmaccadam when muddy tracks were the only roads, it was not unknown for a bogged down cart to be completely abandoned. When this happened, other carts would simply drive a new route around the unfortunate vehicle. This is why so many of our tracks divide and join at regular intervals.* If in doubt of which path to follow, simply keep to the direction of the yellow arrows, painted at regular intervals on tree trunks.

After a short distance, the path becomes far more prominent and you should keep to it, ignoring all turnings off, to later descend into a valley. Ignore a marked footpath off to your right at this point (path number "51") and continue ahead to shortly after, ignore a second marked footpath (path number "50"), this time on your left. You will soon arrive at a junction of paths where you should, as before, carry straight on, still following the yellow arrows painted on tree trunks and now also footpath number "48". The path is now much narrower and runs along the top of a low bank, part of the ancient Grims Ditch.

Grims Ditch (OS. 737843 Map 175) *is one of several similar earthworks in the area. They are mostly of Celtic origin and it is believed acted as boundaries, often stretching for hundreds of miles. The name "Grim" is given to many ancient earthworks such as Grimes Graves (neolithic flint mines in Norfolk), and is associated with the devil as well as representing Woden, the Norse god of warriors. Later, the bank here became the route of the Henley to Wallingford road, though this ended when the turnpike route along the Fairmile opened in 1736. Today, it is simply a footpath.*   *i*

The wood here is especially beautiful, particularly in spring and autumn where you may also be lucky enough to catch sight of a Muntjac deer. On reaching a prominent crossing path (path number "32"), turn left along it, once again ignoring all turnings off.

After going over a crossing path the path, you are on follows the line of a field on your left, before once again cutting through the centre of the wood. Your way here is quite clear, but if in doubt simply follow the yellow arrows. Eventually, the wood ends and the path meets a lane beside a house, "Broadplat Croft". Cross the lane and join a drive almost opposite (slightly to the left), marked as a public footpath and also signposted to Forge Works. After approximately twenty metres, leave the drive and go over a stile on your left and thereafter, turn left to join a signposted footpath which runs between a field on your left and some farm buildings on your right.

As the farm buildings end, cross a stile on your left into a field and then turn right to follow a track along the edge of the field. Soon after, ignore a marked footpath on your right which leads through a gate and continue ahead to go over a wooden plank walkway, constructed to save walkers from wet feet when the pond on your left floods. At the far side of the field, go over another stile and maintain your route along the edge of the next field. On nearing the far side of this field, you will see the old 14th century tower of "Greys Court", ahead to your right.

At the field end cross a stile and carry straight on, heading for the National Trust oriental style ticket office, passing to the left of a brick maze.

The Archbishop's Maze (OS. 726835 Map 175) *was designed for Lady Brunner in 1981. Its inspiration came from a speech given by Dr. Robert Runcie at his enthronement as Archbishop of Canterbury in 1980. In part of his speech, Dr. Runcie expressed his wish that all people should try and solve the secret of the maze of life. The maze is based upon Christian symbolism, a style which became very popular during the Middle Ages, with many Continental churches incorporating a tiled Maze*   *i* *of Life in their floors. Turf mazes, more popular in England, are in some cases, uniquely styled leading to speculation that these in particular, pre-date Christianity.*

The maze path which leads to a central armillary sundial, incredibly for the size of the maze, is a quarter of a mile in length. Along the way the path makes many twists and turns, each having its own meaning and meeting a number of Christian symbols. Finally, it arrives at the sundial which represents the maze for humanity and for eternity. One last note, please respect the maze and do not climb over the fence to gain a better look.

On reaching a tarmac drive to the house, turn right to follow it passing the National Trust Oriental style ticket office. This is a lovely part of the walk with "Greys Court" on your right and a picturesque landscaped valley on the left. If you are a National Trust member or wish to pay for a one-off visit, then it is well worth stopping to tour the house.

i **Greys Court, N.T. (OS. 725834 Map 175)** *takes its name from its original builders, the once powerful de Grey family. The family, already powerful, rose to prominence during the reign of Edward I, Sir Robert de Grey playing an important role in helping Edward to defeat the Welsh. The de Grey's, along with other barons, opposed the weak Edward II and welcomed the ascension of Edward III. Sir John de Grey, Robert's son, went on to help Edward III to defeat the French at Crecy, for which he was made the first Lord de Grey and given permission to fortify "Greys Court".*

Four of the original five towers and some of the wall of the original fortification still remain intact and create a romantic image far removed from their original intent. The last member of the de Grey family disappeared (probably killed, though this has never been proved), after the Battle of Bosworth in 1485, at which King Richard III died. The house and estate consequently passed to the Crown, in this case Henry VII.

Twentynine years later, Henry VII granted the estate to Robert Knollys, a court official. Henry VIII confirmed the estate to Robert's son, Francis, who later married a niece of Anne Boleyn. Francis was a close friend of Henry VIII and after his death, became a close advisor to Elizabeth I who often visited "Greys Court". Having strongly supported Henry VIII in his dispute with the Catholic church, Francis was given the task by Elizabeth I of overseeing the captivity of Mary Queen of Scots at Bolton. He did this between 1568 and 1569 and during that time, became a good friend of Queen Mary and was, no doubt, sad to see her eventual fate.

In 1572, Elizabeth I further rewarded Francis by appointing him Treasurer of the Royal Household - not always a popular position. Francis had seven sons and it was his second son, William, who inherited "Greys Court". After this, the house was sold on several occasions until in 1969, it finally came into the hands of the National Trust in the form of a gift from Sir Felix Brunner, BT.

Though damaged in the Civil War, much of the house built by the Knollys from the original de Grey fortifications, remains today. Still intact and of particular interest, is the old donkey wheel which up until early this century, was used to draw water. Being home and host to so many colourful characters it is surprising that the house has no associated ghosts, though there is a tragic legend. This tells of a bride who on her wedding night as part of the festivities, joined in a game of hide and seek. Whilst hiding she mistakenly locked herself into a large chest. Unable to find her, the distraught groom and guests supposed she had been a reluctant bride and had run off. It was only generations later that her skeleton was found, still in the chest. The story is probably basically true, though whether or not it happened at "Greys Court" is another matter, as a similar story is associated with several Oxfordshire houses, most notably "Minster Lovell". It is commonly known as "The Mistletoe Bough" story.

Follow the drive past the house, ignoring any turnings off to the right. After the house, the drive descends and you should keep to it until it bends left just before reaching a lane. Here you should follow a path ahead to, after a few paces, cross a stile, then a lane and thereafter, another stile the other side into a field. Go straight across the field traversing a shallow valley, obviously popular with moles, and at the far side go over a stile to thereafter, maintain your route, now going uphill through woodland. It is only a short time until you reach the top, where at the same time the woodland ends and the path arrives at a small field with a derelict barn.

Continue ahead, passing to the left of the barn, to soon arrive at the pretty hamlet of Greys Green, with the cricket green directly ahead. Bear right to skirt the edge of the green and pass to the left of the Reg Frewin pavilion and continue until you meet a track beside "Greys Cottage" on your right. Turn right here along the track (do not join the road), passing a second attractive property and continue to pass through a small gate beside a larger one. You should carry straight on, now following a fenced path between fields.

At a second gate there is a small fence gap through which you should pass (if you are thin!) to enter a small beech wood, Sams Wood. The path immediately forks and you should carry straight on along path number "22", keeping to the left hand edge of the wood. At the far side of the wood, the path continues between fields where you will shortly meet a stile which you should cross. Thereafter, carry straight on along the left hand perimeter of a field and on nearing the far side, cross another stile to follow a fenced path around the perimeter of a garden. The path soon leads out to the beautiful hamlet of Shepherds Green (no prizes for guessing the origin of this hamlet's name). As with Greys Green, the hamlet is dotted with pretty cottages encircling a small green, including one delightful thatched property straight out of a Grims fairy tale.

Turn left onto the track which runs across the centre of the green and almost immediately after (a few paces), turn right onto a gravel track passing to the left of a lovely rambling cottage, "The Strip". As the track bends right to enter a second property, you should leave it to continue ahead to soon arrive at a stile in between two gates. Go over the stile into a field and turn left to follow the field perimeter behind more houses belonging to Shepherds Green. There are good views behind to your right here to Pissen Wood, which encircles the hill behind "Greys Court".

At the far side of the field, go over a stile and continue straight across the next field heading for the right hand perimeter of a copse in view ahead. On reaching the copse maintain your route, keeping to the field perimeter, with the copse on your left. At the far side of the field cross a stile beside a gate and go straight across the next field, heading for a stile visible the other side. Go over this stile to enter an area of yet more typical Chiltern beech woodland, Padnell's Wood, where in spring the floor is a carpet of bluebells.

Continue ahead and after a few paces, fork right (in the direction of a white arrow) along a narrow path to shortly reach a wide crossing path. Turn right onto the crossing path which quickly narrows and continues through the wood slowly bending left. Soon it meets another path onto which you should turn right, thereby maintaining your route ahead. Ignore all turnings off to soon arrive at a lane **(OS**

707839). Cross the lane and go over a stile to join a signposted footpath the other side which crosses the centre of a field, at the far side of which you should go over two stiles in quick succession to enter another wood, Holly Grove.

The path continues ahead through dense fir woodland to soon meet a track. Turn right along the track and after approximately thirty metres, left onto a narrow path marked by a white arrow (take care not to miss it). The path leads through lovely mixed woodland which has been left for self generation and in my opinion, is all the better for it. Considering its name, there are a distinct lack of holly bushes but there are some magnificent laurels. Sometime later, the path meets another track onto which you should turn left and after approximately twenty metres when the track bends left, you should leave it to carry straight on in the direction of the white arrows. The going is somewhat undefined here but if you keep to the white arrows you should not lose your way.

To reassure you, the path soon meets and follows the line of a field on your left and at the same time, you should ignore a crossing path. After a short distance the path bears right, away from the field, heading back into the wood. A little later, you will pass to the left of a large crater and shortly after, you should ignore a marked footpath off to the right (white arrow), continuing ahead to soon arrive at a road, the B481, onto which you should turn right. This, in turn, will lead you to "The Dog and Duck", Brakspear's, at Highmoor. At the time of writing, the current tenants of "The Carpenters Arms" at Crockers End are about to take over the tenancy of "The Dog and Duck". This should mean the same friendly hospitality will continue at "The Dog and Duck", with the added attraction of an extensive and imaginative menu to compliment the excellent Brakspear's ales. Opposite the pub is the distinctive "Yew Tree Cottage", with its yew tree carved in the shape of a duck - where's the dog?

Pass in front of the pub and continue along the road, ignoring a marked bridleway off to the right. Approximately twenty metres on, cross the road to join a signposted footpath on your left, which leads up a short drive before going over a stile to the right of the drive, just in front of the beautiful "Appletree Cottage". Continue, now following the left hand perimeter of a field, to soon cross a stile at the far side and enter a small copse full of holly bushes. As you enter the copse, fork right and follow a well trodden path through its centre to soon arrive at a crossing path in front of a lovely converted barn.

Go over the crossing path and continue ahead for a few paces before bending right to follow a narrow path which runs through a strip of woodland, dominated by laurels, in front of the converted barn mentioned. At the far end, go over a stile leaving the wood and continue, now following the right hand perimeter of a small field, to shortly meet and cross a second stile. This takes you into a larger field where you should maintain your route, keeping to the right hand perimeter, with find views ahead.

At the far side of the field, go over a stile and bear gently diagonally left across the next field, descending the steep side of a beautiful valley. At the bottom, known as Stony Bottom, cross another stile into yet another field and head up the other side of the valley, going gently diagonally left across the field heading for a stile at the far side. As a guide, the stile is approximately fifty metres in from the right hand corner.

Cross the stile and then a second quickly after, to enter the next field where you should cross the field, again bearing gently diagonally left, heading just to the right of a house visible ahead to your left. As you progress, on a clear day, there are views left to the hills in Berkshire the other side of the Thames valley. At the far side, go over a stile to meet a track onto which you should turn left. After passing two houses on the left the track descends gradually and later bends right in front of a lovely decorative brick and timber cottage. (Ignore a marked footpath off to the right which leads behind the cottage). When the track forks, keep right following the perimeter of the cottage grounds, to soon arrive at a narrow lane.

Cross the lane and carry straight on along a signposted public bridleway to soon after, meet a second lane which you should again cross. Join a footpath the other side and follow this as it immediately bends right (in the direction of a yellow arrow) ignoring a marked bridleway (blue arrow) leading straight on. On meeting a fork, keep right thereby continuing ahead to, a few paces on, go over a crossing path maintaining your route uphill. Shortly after, the path follows the line of a field on your right and as you continue, a picturesque white painted house will come into view the other side.

The path eventually comes out at the driveway to the white house mentioned and you should turn left along it to soon meet a lane. Turn right along the lane to arrive at the second pub on our walk, "The Crooked Billet", Brakspear's, at Stoke Row. This pub, in my opinion, is one of the best in the Chilterns and certainly serves the best food, perfect for a special occasion. If you need a reason to celebrate, you have just reached the highest point on our walk. "The Crooked Billet" also marks the half way point. The pub is certainly an experience to remember and has been well preserved avoiding modernisation. It does not even have a bar, a bar being a relatively modern custom.

From the pub it is possible to make a short detour to visit the Maharajah's Well. To do this, follow the lane past the pub to arrive at the main road which passes through the centre of the village. Turn right and you will soon arrive at the well. You will need to retrace your steps back to the pub to continue our walk.

The Maharajah's Well, Stoke Row (OS. 677841 Map 175) *was a gift from the Maharajah of Benares. He had never visited Stoke Row but wished to repay his friend, Edward Reade of Ipsden, Lieutenant Govenor of India's North West Provinces, for his support during the Indian mutiny. The Maharajah recalled a conversation with Mr. Reade ten years earlier about the lack of water at Stoke Row and how hard it was for the people living there. The Maharajah thus found the ideal way to repay his friend and the country which had given him support.*

The well was started in 1863 and was dug by hand to a depth of 368 feet, an incredible feat when you consider the well is only 4 feet wide. The publicity leaflet helps picture this by comparing it with two Nelson's columns, one on top of the other. It certainly helps to focus the mind. The Maharajah also paid for a cherry orchard beside the well, with proceeds from the annual sale of the cherries going towards the

*upkeep of the well. Today, the cherry
orchard is open for the public to enjoy.
The village also has a pub, "The
Cherry Tree", Brakspear's, named
after the orchard.*

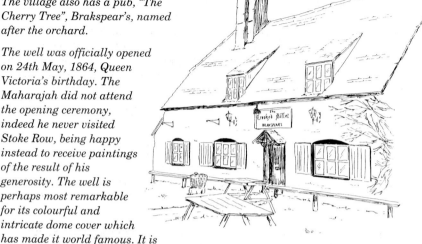

*The well was officially opened
on 24th May, 1864, Queen
Victoria's birthday. The
Maharajah did not attend
the opening ceremony,
indeed he never visited
Stoke Row, being happy
instead to receive paintings
of the result of his
generosity. The well is
perhaps most remarkable
for its colourful and
intricate dome cover which
has made it world famous. It is
also remarkable for supporting a continued and valued friendship between the people
of this remote Chiltern village and the current Maharajah of Benares.*

To continue our walk from, "The Crooked Billet", retrace your steps along the lane.
This time ignore the drive way on the left by which you arrived and keep to the lane
until it bends right, where you should leave it to continue ahead along a marked
bridleway (blue arrow). Do not make the mistake of taking the bridleway which
leads left downhill.

The bridleway runs in a straight line along the top of a valley side and also along
the edge of Bush Wood. It is fairly well walked but if in doubt, there are white
arrows on the tree trunks to guide your way. You should ignore any turnings off and
keep to the edge of the wood (at a marked fork, keeping right), to eventually, after a
short descent, arrive at a lane beside a house on your right. Cross the lane and join
a signposted public bridleway the other side which leads uphill through Bear Wood,
the name being a reminder of the animal which once roamed these extensive woods.
Bear Wood is the largest expanse of woodland which we traverse on today's walk.

Although the bridleway is fairly well used, at certain times of the year the maze of
animal tracks can make the going confusing. It is important therefore, that you
follow the white arrows painted on tree trunks at regular intervals. Later, the
bridleway crosses the head of a shallow valley and, as a guide, you should just be
able to make out, through the trees, a large modern white house to your right. From
here the bridleway follows a bank for a few paces before plunging into the depths of
Bear Wood once more.

The bridleway eventually meets a crossing path marked by white arrows, where you
should turn right for a few paces to pass between some wooden posts. After the
posts turn immediately left and follow a prominent path along the edge of a pine
plantation known as Burnt Platt Wood. Keep to the path which sometime later
descends to meet a wide crossing track beside two Forestry Commission signs, one
for Burnt Platt Wood and the other for Greyhone Wood (**OS. 696833**).

Go straight over the crossing track and join a bridleway the other side, marked by a blue arrow, which leads through the centre of Greyhone Wood. Do not be tempted to turn right into the wood beside a "No Horses" sign. The bridleway which is in the form of a track, follows a low bank on your right, another ancient boundary. Sometime later, it appears to fork and at this point you should descend the bank on your right, thereby taking the right hand fork, to pass a post with a horseshoe on it. If you find yourself suddenly bending sharp left, you know you have missed the fork. The bridleway now begins to descend becoming steeper as you go. In wet weather this route can be very slippery so great care is needed.

On reaching the bottom, turn right at a "T" junction along what can be a very muddy path. The path which is well used, proceeds along the bottom of a valley running parallel with another bank, this one being on your left. Later the path twists through the bank after which it again runs parallel with the bank, now on your right. Eventually, the path arrives at a wide crossing track, which you should ignore thereby maintaining your route ahead along the valley bottom. The path is now more a track and in wet weather is often even muddier! I do hope you have those boots on.

Ignore all further turnings off and follow the track along the valley bottom for approximately half a mile, where the track leaves the wood to continue between fields. This is but a short interlude and it is not long before the track enters woodland once more (ignore a track off to the left), though this time it is only a narrow strip, appropriately named Littlebottom Wood. If the track is too muddy there is a well walked path running parallel on your left to assist your progress. You will eventually arrive at a lane on a bend and small parking area.

Continue ahead along the lane and after a short distance when it bends left, leave it to follow a narrower lane ahead. This takes you past a parking area before reaching a main road, the B481, at Rotherfield Peppard.

Rotherfield Peppard (OS. 709817 Map 175) *is a scattered village encircling a large common. Indeed, the name "Rotherfield", of Saxon origin, means "open land for grazing". "Peppard" is dervied from the Lord of the manor, Ralph Pypard, who was given the estate during the reign of Edward I. The parish of Rotherfield Peppard, like many in this part of the Chilterns (see "Up Flow Down Tow"), stretches in a long thin line to the Thames, in this case to Mill Lane at Henley. In return for access to fresh water, the people of Henley were allowed free grazing rights on the common.*

Rotherfield Peppard is also on the old trading route known as the "Pack and Prime" road, which cut overland from Henley to Goring, carrying goods from the barges which found it difficult to navigate the large loop of the river through Reading. Unfortunately, today, the village straddles another popular route, the B481, which makes peaceful appreciation of the village somewhat testing. Perhaps the best way is to visit one of the village's two hostelries. To do this, turn left across the green to arrive at "The Red Lion", Brakspear's. A little further on, is "The Dog", Morland, which, unlike "The Red Lion", is open all day for food and drink. If you visit either of these pubs, to continue the route simply follow the road opposite "The Red Lion" to reach the village school where you rejoin the official route.

If you have not detoured to the pubs mentioned, cross the B481 and take a path across the green ahead, making for the village school and a red telephone box.

99

On reaching the school, bear right along a lane marked as a dead end and follow it, ignoring all turnings off, to its end where you will arrive at the village church.

i
✝
■
All Saints Church, Rotherfield Peppard (OS. 714816 Map 175) *dates from the 12th century and was probably built by the Pypard family. It is a peaceful and simple church positioned at the end of the village, which has gradually moved to remain near the main trade routes. Inside, the most notable feature are the three original 12th century windows, their size affording only minimal light.*

From the lane end, follow a track which passes to the right of the church, ignoring a signposted footpath off to the right, and when the track proceeds to enter a property ahead, leave it to go over a stile on your left. Thereafter, follow a fenced footpath between fields where you should look out for the large red brick Victorian rectory on your left. You are now in an area offering open views, a pleasant change to the miles of walking through woodland which can, at times, be quite claustrophobic.

Go over a stile into a large field and bear gently left, following a prominent path across the centre of the field. On reaching an oak tree at the centre, bear gently right and head for a stile now visible at the far side. Cross the stile to enter a wood known as The Paddock and turn left onto a crossing path which runs along the edge of the wood. The path later bends right and then left before arriving at a crossing track (the old "Pack and Prime" road), after passing through a metal gate. Turn right along the track to shortly arrive at a junction of tracks, where you should turn left passing through a small wooden gate beside a metal one.

Your way is now along one of the very ancient routes which have criss-crossed the Chilterns for centuries. The track is bordered by thick hedgerows and in spring dotted with snowdrops. Continue until you see a stile on your right which you should cross (take care not to miss it) and carry straight on across the left hand corner of a field. Visible in the distance on your left is the village of Greys Green, passed earlier on our walk. At the far side of the field, go over a large stile and continue across the centre of the next field, making for the church at the hamlet of Rotherfield Greys ahead. At the field end, cross another stile and follow a path which runs alongside the churchyard wall, to arrive at a lane beside the last pub on our route before arriving back at Henley, "The Malsters Arms", Brakspear's. Welcome to Rotherfield Greys.

i
✝
■
Y
▟
Rotherfield Greys (OS. 726824 Map 175), *like Rotherfield Peppard, is named after the original Lord of the manor, in this case Lord de Grey, first encountered on our walk at "Greys Court". It is the village church built in the 13th century by the de Grey family, which most people come to see. Inside, are two magnificent memorials to men who have helped shape the history of our land. The first is a superb brass to Lord Robert de Grey, a founder Knight of the Garter. The second is the Knollys Chapel which houses an ornately carved and colourful memorial to the Knollys family. The carving depicts Sir Francis Knollys and his wife, Catherine, with a child at her side that died in infancy. Although Sir Francis lies here, Elizabeth I had Catherine buried at Westminster Abbey as befitting a close relative of the Queen. It was Francis' second son, William, who paid for the chapel. From all accounts however, he was not a particularly likeable character but was certainly colourful and, it is believed, was used by Shakespeare on which to base his character, Malvolio, in "Twelfth Night".*

There is one rather unusual story associated with the church. This relates to the Reverend J. Ingram who, in 1823, to raise money, cultivated a small field n⸱⸱⸱⸱⸱

church to grow the white poppy for opium. Although, apparently, it was of extremely high quality and fetched a good price, it did not cover the Reverend's costs and the idea was abandoned, though not before he was awarded a silver medal by the Society of Arts and Sciences for his method in collecting the opium. I should quickly add that the village does not include opium amongst its crops today!

Opposite the church stands an ornate shelter with a plaque stating that it was erected in 1897 in commemoration of the Queen's Diamond Jubilee. Originally built as a well cover it has since served as the village shop and most recently as a bus shelter. The village pub is one not to be missed. Its name, "The Malsters Arms", refers to the trade of malting, common to the area in the 17th and 18th centuries.

To continue our walk, turn right along the lane passing between the church and the ornate shelter opposite. After the shelter, turn left through a kissing gate to enter a field where you should join a signposted public footpath which forks right, marked "Henley 2½ miles". Follow the field perimeter which runs behind some gardens, also passing through an avenue of trees. As the gardens end, you should maintain your route through the avenue of trees to shortly follow the right hand field perimeter down the side of a valley where there are glorious views left towards "Greys Court". At the valley bottom, go over a stile on your right and continue ahead along the left hand perimeter of the next field.

After a short distance, go over a stile on your left into another field (take care not to miss it) and turn right to follow the field perimeter. After a short distance, go over another stile into the next field and continue ahead (ignore a marked path off to the left) along the right hand perimeter of this field. At the far side, cross yet another stile and carry straight on along a track which leads down from an avenue of horse chestnut trees on your right. The track, at first, acts as a dividing line between fields and after going over a crossing track, runs along the edge of a copse on your left known as Ash Plantation.

When Ash Plantation ends the track forks and you should take the right hand fork thereby maintaining your route ahead. You will shortly meet a stile to the right of a 17th century farmhouse, "Lower Hernes", which you should cross to continue ahead across a partly wooded field. At the far side, go over another stile into the next field and carry straight on along the right hand perimeter, following the bottom of Hernes valley. *The name "Hernes" could mean "grey valley" or refer to "Hern", the hunter and forester to Richard II. He was known to frequently visit these parts and there are several stories of his ghost which appears in human form wearing the skull of a stag.*

The field is a long one and if you are tired it can seem an age before you reach the far side. When you do, go over a stile, cross a crossing path (the last time we meet the "Pack and Prime" road) and then go over another stile to follow a fenced path the other side. It is not long before the path passes to the left of some playing fields which are part of Henley College, an early sign that you are nearing Henley and the end of our walk.

The path eventually bends left and arrives at a kissing gate beside some tennis courts on your left and suddenly, before you, the Henley suburbs come into view. Pass through the kissing gate and continue ahead, passing to the right of a parking area. Thereafter, cross a lane and join a tarmac path the other side and as this bends left to go up some steps, you should leave it to continue ahead along another path, which, at the time of writing, is gravel but maybe tarmacked in the future.

The path you have joined soon leads out to a lane beside a tile hung house and you should continue ahead along the lane to shortly arrive at a road, Paradise Road. Follow the road ahead (do not turn right), to shortly meet another road in front of the entrance to "Friar Park".

i **Friar Park (OS. 755827 Map 175)** *which is private, is the home of ex-Beatle, George Harrison. The house was built in 1896 by a solicitor, Frank Crisp, and is of a bizarre gothic style. Mr. Crisp was something of a child at heart and had the grounds landscaped to satisfy his childhood fantasies. This meant constructing a minature version of the Swiss Alps as well as underground caverns and lakes. In the various caverns he placed working models such as a crocodile and a skeleton which moved and lit up. They were some of the earliest amusements powered by electricity in the country. George Harrison is believed to have invested considerably in having these models and amusements restored. To protect his privacy, there is no public access.*

Cross the road, turn right and after a few paces take a one-way street ahead to retrace your steps back into Henley town centre, our starting point. Henley, because of its history, boasts a wealth of pubs in which you can celebrate your completion of the walk. On other walks I have suggested that if you find it hard to choose, celebrate in them all. Doing this at Henley however, could not only take several days but probably result in a visit to the local hospital! It would be unfair to recommend any one pub in particular - the decision must be yours.

i **Henley on Thames (OS. 760826 Map 175)** *is an attractive and complex town and of course, the home of rowing. For centuries, Henley was an important port on the Thames and with the building of a solid bridge, became an equally important stop on coaching routes. Henley's Thames frontage is probably the most famous and picturesque part of the town. It is also where the Henley Royal Regatta takes place. The modern building on the far bank opposite "The Angel" pub, is the Royal Regatta headquarters. It replaced the 18th century "Carpenters Arms" and was designed by Terry Farrell, famous or some would say infamous, for designing TV AM's building at Camden Lock in London.*

The bridge across the Thames, as mentioned at the start of the walk, was built in 1787. The faces on the keystones over the central arch represent the Thames and the Isis. Horace Walpole, the writer, described the bridge as "the most beautiful in the world after the Ponti di Trinita at Florence". Beautiful the bridge certainly is, but this opinion is I believe, an exaggeration and probably tinged with bias as it was Mr. Walpole's cousin, the Honorable Mrs. Damer, who was responsible for some of the sculptures on the bridge.

Stand on the bridge for just a few minutes and you will see at least one rowing team at practice. The long narrow boats with oarsmen in perfect unison are as much a part of the Thames as the hungry swans and ducks. Indeed, it is hard to imagine this stretch of the Thames having ever been without them. In fact, the opposite is true. Although Henley staged the first University boat race in 1829, rowing on this part of the Thames was a hazardous business. In the 18th and early 19th centuries, the Thames was choked with working barges, some so large that they required as many as fourteen horses to pull them. It was not until the arrival of the railway in the mid-19th century, that the river traffic declined and competition rowing became popular.

In 1839, the Regatta was established and with the Prince Consort's patronage in 1851, it acquired its royal status making it to this day one of the great society events of the year.

River apart, Henley has many other charms including buildings of interest, far too numerous to detail here. The church which dates from the 14th century is worth a visit and if you are staying in the area, so is the Kenton Theatre, reputed to be the second oldest in the country. "The Red Lion Hotel", is also worth a visit to sample the atmosphere as well as the local brew. Built in the 16th century, it has played host to a wealth of notable visitors, including Charles I, Prince Rupert, the Prince Regent (to watch the Regatta) and the Duke of Wellington. It was in "The Red Lion Hotel" that I raised my glass to an adventure that acquainted me with a baron's castle, an Indian well, an opium growing Reverend and the home of an ex-Beatle as well as a few excellent hostelries. Which one will you remember and toast most?

ACCOMMODATION
Henley has a wealth of accommodation from the grandest hotel to the modest B&B. For full details, contact the Henley Tourist Information Centre, Town Hall, Market Place, Henley. Tel. 0491 578034.

Slaters Farm, Peppard Common. Tel: 0491 628675

On the walk, this is an extremely comfortable place to stay. One of the highlights is the beautiful garden which includes a tennis court, available to guests.

Youth Hostel, Streatley YHA, Streatley. Tel: 0491 872278

Approximately fifteen miles from the walk, the recently refurbished Streatley hostel now offers small family rooms as well as the normal dorms we all know. The hostel itself is a large Victorian house only a few paces from "The Bull Inn".

Camping and Caravanning, Swiss Farm, Henley. Tel: 0491 573419

Approximately half a mile from the walk, this is a fairly large and busy site close to the Thames.

FOLLOW THE RED BRICK ROAD

Distance: 15 miles (24.14 km)

Time: Allow approximately 8 hours

Map: Ordnance Survey Landranger Map 175

START
WARBURG NATURE RESERVE
100M

EWELME
PARK
180M

EWELME
90M

FINISH
WARBURG NATURE RESERVE
100M

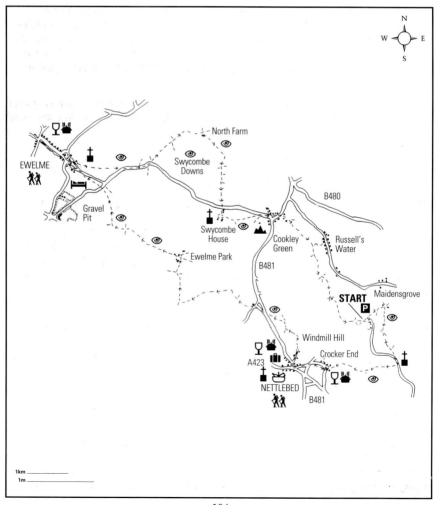

Walk Summary

This is the most challenging walk in the book and in my opinion, the most satisfying. Every step of the way there is something new to see. From woods to fields, along valleys and over hills, through villages and past great houses, Follow the Red Brick Road does it all in style. The scenery is a constant attraction and on occasions you are further spoilt with the reward of some glorious views. Most of the paths are well walked and mud is not as big a problem as with some of the other walks in this book. However, apart from the distance which can be tiring, there are several hard climbs so do not assume you can complete this walk on a Sunday afternoon or after a heavy pub meal. Talking of pubs, there are a number of good hostelries en route, though apart from "The Shepherds Hut" at Ewelme which requires a short detour, they are all during the early stages. With this in mind and assuming you wish to finish, think before you drink!

Start - OS. 721878 Map 175

The walk starts from the BBONT car park at the Warburg Nature Reserve. The easiest way to get there (if there is one) is to join the B480 from the A423 just north of Henley, signposted to Assendons and Stonor. After passing through Middle Assendon, take the narrow road left signposted to Bix Bottom (this is easy to miss so take care) and follow this for approximately two miles, ignoring all turnings off, to reach the car park which is on your right opposite the Visitors Centre. The car park has a gate which is often shut but not locked. Take care not to drive past it thinking it is an entrance to a field.

Alternative starts can be made at Ewelme or Nettlebed. The nearest railway station is at Henley from where it is possible to follow the Oxfordshire Way to join the walk at the reserve (a distance of approximately two miles).

FOLLOW THE RED BRICK ROAD

Starting at the Warburg Nature Reserve, you are starting from one of the most dramatic and remote areas in the Chilterns.

The Warburg Nature Reserve (OS. 721878 Map 175) is named after Dr. E. F. Warburg, a botanist from Oxford University and a Vice President of BBONT (Berkshire, Buckinghamshire and Oxfordshire Naturalists Trust). The reserve protects a remote wooded valley of two hundred and fiftyeight acres and is BBONT's largest and most important reserve. The air at the bottom of the valley is often cool and it is not unusual for the valley to have a frost, even though one is not experienced elsewhere locally. Bear this in mind when making an early start.

Many species of animals, insects and birds live on the reserve, though it is best known for its rich variety of flora of which over four hundred and fifty species of plants have been recorded, including seventeen types of orchid. If you have any energy left at the end of the walk, there is a nature trail which is well worth following and a Visitors Centre where you will find more detailed information on the reserve.

Whilst walking through the reserve (and even when not), please avoid picking any of the flowers. Leave them for others to enjoy.

From the car park, walk away from the entrance to join a track which passes to the left of a small wooden shelter, acting as an information point for the Warburg Nature Reserve. Shortly after, turn right onto a grass path marked as a nature trail and follow it as it bends left, going uphill, passing through woodland to come out at a long strip of grass. Here the path bends left again along the grass strip and passes a nature trail sheep grazing sign, where after a further forty metres you should turn right onto a crossing path, marked as a footpath.

The footpath leads steeply uphill through more woodland which has a rich thick moss covered floor, a pleasant distraction from your fairly strenuous climb. Near the top the path bends right (where there is a lovely view right) and continues over two stiles in quick succession to meet another path. Turn left here, continuing your route uphill, and follow the path which soon levels out to eventually reach a stile at the edge of the sprawling hamlet of Maidensgrove. Cross the stile to immediately meet a track marked as the Oxfordshire Way, onto which you should turn right taking you back into the nature reserve.

The track soon begins a gentle descent and later follows the line of a field on your left, affording good views on the same side across to Great Hill. You should ignore a track on your left here which leads into a field and continue ahead to soon pass a clearing on your right, where trees have been cut down to allow a route for electricity poles. This, in turn, allows a good view up the centre of the nature reserve. Just after this, the track forks and you should continue ahead, taking the right hand fork. This almost immediately starts a steeper descent and becomes fenced, passing through some lovely open woodland.

Near the bottom the track suddenly bursts free of the wood and you can enjoy views of a very different part of the valley, mainly arable though equally attractive. From here, the track is thickly hedged and continues downhill between fields to soon arrive at the lane which leads to the nature reserve. Until the turnpike road was opened, now the A423, this lane was the Watlington to Oxford road. Turn left along the lane to shortly pass the romantic ruin of St. James' church at Bix Bottom.

St. James' Church, Bix Bottom (OS. 726869 Map 175) *is*
a ruin of an originally Norman church. The church served the farming community in the valley until 1875, when it was abandoned with the diverting of the Oxfordshire road to the route of the current A423. A new church was built beside the new road and a community grew up around it, living off the passing trade. This is now Bix village. Despite local legend, there is no evidence that there was ever a village supporting St. James' church.

The church has deteriorated quickly and today, there is really only an ivy clad shell remaining as well as a few gravestones. The picture is however, not displeasing and the ruin blends in well with the valley, being far

The ruined Church - Bix Bottom

106

more romantic than a pristinely preserved building.

Follow the lane past the church and almost immediately after, turn right, thereby leaving the lane and the Oxfordshire Way, onto a track marked as a public footpath to Crocker End. This leads up the other side of the valley along the left hand perimeter of a field, where on nearing the top and at the far end of the field, you should pass through a gate and follow a track ahead into Wellgrove Wood. At first the track follows the line of a field on your left and here you have lovely views left down through the valley to the appropriately named "Valley Farm".

After this, the track runs through the centre of Wellgrove Wood where soon after entering, you should ignore a track off to the left. Continue ahead to pass through a beautiful area of beech woodland and as you walk look out for a low oblong pit beside the track. This was once a saw pit.

Saw pits *were used when cutting trees into logs or planks. Two men used a large double handed saw to cut tree trunks down to size. One would saw standing in the pit with the other sawing from above. The position standing in the pit was not an enviable one and was often done by an apprentice who would be called an "under dog". The man standing above was known as the "top dog". These two expressions have stayed with us even though the practice from which they were derived is long gone.*

Another current every-day expression, "bodge job", also stems from the woodmans trade. Bodgers were people who roughly worked wood into a saleable size and shape for the carpenter. Their skill was limited and carpenters often looked down upon their work, despite the fact that it saved them considerable labour. Consequently, a poorly made piece of furniture was often referred to as "a bodger's" or "bodge job". This term has been extended today to apply to any badly finished or temporary job.

Sometime later, ignore another track off to the left and a second off to the right almost immediately after. Again, you should maintain your route ahead to follow what is now more a path which runs along the edge of a yew plantation on the right.

Eventually, the path reaches the other side of the wood where you should go over a stile and continue ahead along the left hand side of a field and also along the top of a valley overlooked by the imposing "Soundess House", ahead to your right. Keep to the field perimeter which slowly bends left, where the first houses of Crocker End will come into view ahead. At the far side of the field, go over a stile beside a gate and turn right along a track to enter the lovely rambling village of Crocker End. Crocker End is so called as it was once part of the brick and pottery industry centred around Nettlebed, our next destination.

The track soon arrives at a lane in front of the village green, onto which you should turn left to reach our first pub, "The Carpenters Arms", Brakspear's. Even though you are expecting it, because of its hidden position, the pub is still a surprise. It is another excellent Brakspear's hostelry and one that preserves the ideal of the local pub. Sadly, at the time of writing, the pub is in danger of closure and I hope by the time you walk this way, you do not find yet another pub converted into a private house.

Follow the lane round in front of the pub, ignorning a lane off to the left, thereby doing a complete horseshoe to arrive back at the village green. Here you should leave t' e lane to take a footpath on your left, signposted to Nettlebed. The path 1 ng one the left hand side of the green which is loosely bordered by half timbered houses and traditional Chiltern flint and brick cottages, to later meet the lane once more. Turn left to follow the lane and shortly after, ignore two other lanes off to the right and left respectively and carry straight on to soon pass the first houses of Nettlebed.

Stay on the lane to arrive at the village green with the noisy A423/A4130 on your left at the far side of the green. Continue to soon arrive at a small modern housing development on the right, The Old Kiln, at the centre of which is an old brick kiln.

Nettlebed (OS. 702867 Map 175). *The brick kiln is a monument to Nettlebed's past, for until recently Nettlebed was the local centre of a brick making industry dating back to the 14th century. The earliest order can be traced as far back as 1365, this being tiles for Wallingford Castle. Many of the houses in this part of the Chilterns are made from Nettlebed bricks including the famous "Stonor House", visited on "The Christmas Cracker". The local clay and plentiful wood for fuel made Nettlebed the obvious choice for brick making.*

At the industry's height in the mid-19th century, Nettlebed boasted five kilns. The present kiln known as a bottle kiln because of its shape, was the last to stop working in 1938. When in use it held up to twelve thousand bricks at one time.

The Kiln - Nettlebed

The rest of the village straddles the A4130, the old Roman road between London and Oxford. The village church is at the western end of the village. This is relatively modern and usually locked, so hardly worth the detour unless you wish to see the site of Nettlebed's earliest known kiln which stood beside the church.

For refreshments, Nettlebed has a general stores as well as two hostelries. My favourite is "The White Hart Hotel" on the A4130. "The White Hart Hotel" was once a popular coaching inn where Queen Elizabeth I is reputed to have stayed. Today, it has preserved its character with exposed beams, a real fire and traditional furnishings. The food is excellent and very reasonably priced and there is also a good selection of real ales. Nettlebed's other hostelry is "The Sun Inn", Brakspear's. This is a small cosy pub with one of the biggest collections of jugs I have ever seen. There is a roaring fire in winter which makes stopping here very tempting. The food is basic but well prepared and the portions are good. Considering this is the last pub en route without making a detour, you may wish to seriously think about stocking up!

After The Old Kiln housing estate, leave the lane and continue along a tarmac path ahead to pass through some metal railings into Watlington Street. Turn right pass "The Sun Inn" and just after, turn right again onto a track, a signposted bridleway also marked as Mill Road, beside the lovely "Pottery Cottage". Ignore any turnings off and follow the track past a large white house and a pair of brick Victorian cottages, after which the track forks. Take the left hand fork thereby maintaining your route ahead, to now begin your ascent of Windmill Hill.

At the top of the hill, the track passes to the left of a lovely weatherboarded cottage, once the cottage serving a windmill on this site, after which it ends beside a small underground reservoir on the right. When the track ends, take a prominent path off to the left which almost immediately forks. Take the right hand fork to start your descent of the northern side of the hill. To your left are a multitude of small pits and mounds, further remains of the old brick making industry. As you descend, the path is criss-crossed by a maze of smaller paths. You should ignore these and ensure you keep to the official footpath which bears gently right and is marked by white arrows on tree trunks.

Stay on the path to go over a number of crossing paths, keeping in the direction of the white arrows, to soon arrive at a track, well used by motor vehicles, onto which you should turn right. The track leads gently downhill where you should look out, soon after joining (approximately thirty metres), for a prominent but unmarked crossing path onto which you should turn left. (If you arrive at a couple of houses, one relatively modern, then you will have gone too far and should retrace your steps to find the correct route). The path runs parallel with a tree-lined bank on your right, an old boundary, and later meets a more prominent path joining from the left where you should carry straight on, still with the bank on your right.

Sometime on, the path loops around a fallen tree where you should keep bearing right to rejoin the bank and thereafter, continue to arrive at a track. Turn right along the track and after approximately fifteen paces, turn left onto a path marked by a white arrow (do not take the path which follows the bank). You will now follow a narrow path which winds gently through woodland. After a short distance, you should ignore another narrow path off to the right, although it is worth making a detour of just a few paces along it to reach a stile and enjoy wonderful views across to Devil's Hill and Russells Water. This is a lovely spot for an early rest from which you must retrace your steps to rejoin our route.

Ignore any further turnings off and keep to the main path, which eventually bends left to meet another path running parallel with the tree-lined bank you were following earlier. Turn right here along the path with the tree-lined bank now on your left, to shortly arrive at a road, the B481 **(OS. 694880)**. Cross the road and turn right along the grass verge the other side and after a few paces, turn left along a narrow lane in front of a couple of pretty cottages. This leads to another lane onto which you should turn left to follow it for approximately fifteen metres, where you should leave it as it bends left beside a house on your right, "Digberry Farm". You should now follow a track ahead, signposted as a bridleway, to later pass another house, "Gannock Cottage".

The track ends at a third house where you should continue ahead along a marked bridleway which winds through a strip of woodland. You should ignore all turnings off to eventually meet a path (also a bridleway) joining from the right, onto which you should bear left, thereby maintaining your route ahead. After a few paces you will arrive at a wide crossing track, a farm track giving access to fields either side of the wood. Go over the crossing track and follow the path ahead to shortly arrive at a marked footpath (white arrow) leading off to the right in front of a pair of metal posts. Turn right along the footpath, in the direction of the white arrow numbered "NU14", and follow it downhill to meet a crossing path.

Turn left along the crossing path, also marked by a white arrow as well as "NU7". The footpath which can be very muddy in wet weather, descends gradually through Hazel Wood, the floor of which in spring is a carpet of bluebells. You should ignore any turnings off and keep to the main path at all times to eventually pass through a small wooden gate, after which the wood narrows. Maintain your route ahead to later arrive at a prominent crossing path, the Ridgeway, a National Trail (see "Taming the Lions"), identified by the white acorn on posts either side of the wood.

Turn right along the Ridgeway, thereby leaving the woodland, to cross the centre of a large field in the direction of a yellow arrow and white acorn. If the field has just been ploughed and the way is unclear, head for a white post which is visible (as long as there is no famous Chiltern mist!) the other side. As you progress, on a clear day there are good views left across the plain to the futuristic looking Didcot Power Station and the escarpment of the Berkshire Downs which carries the Ridgeway towards Avebury in Wiltshire. At the far side, go over a crossing track passing to the right of the white post mentioned and continue to follow a tree-lined path ahead. This shortly meets a track which you should join to continue ahead.

A few paces after, the Ridgeway passes to the left of a pond, immediately after which you should fork right along a track, still marked as the Ridgeway. As you progress, to your left there are more superb views across the plain and to Didcot. Soon after, the track passes to the right of a large house, "Ewelme Park" **(OS. 674893)**. The house was built in 1913 and is a poor copy of the original Elizabethan house which was destroyed by fire. On meeting the driveway to the property, carry straight on (do not turn right along the drive) passing to the right of the gatehouse. Thereafter, follow a track ahead to soon meet a crossing track, marked as a bridleway.

Turn left onto the bridleway, thereby leaving the Ridgeway, and pass between a white cottage on your left and stables on the right. Thereafter, keep to the bridleway as it descends following the line of a field on your left, to later pass a pond on your right. This is well hidden, especially in summer, so keep your eyes peeled. You will later arrive at a junction of tracks in front of two fields where you should enter the right hand field to continue ahead along the left hand perimeter (do not turn right). You will initially pass to the left of an area of newly planted trees.

As you descend there are now lovely views ahead to the edge of Chiltern country and beyond across the plain. At the far side of the field, pass through a small gateway and carry straight on along the right hand perimeter of the next field. After a short distance, the perimeter fencing of the field gives way on your right and the bridleway becomes the dividing line between two fields. A word of warning - the bridleway is well used by horses and in wet weather can be extremely muddy and churned up to make walking difficult. I do hope you are wearing those boots!

Eventually, you will arrive at a junction of tracks, a crossroads, marked by a wooden post and several blue arrows. Go over the junction and continue ahead following a track along the left hand perimeter of a field. The track soon becomes fenced and hedged on your right and ascends gradually affording marvellous views right across to Swyncombe Down. As the field on your right ends you should take a track right marked by a blue arrow, known locally as Grindon Lane (a Saxon name which means "track over a green hill"), one of the old drovers routes. The track, bordered by ancient hedgerows, descends gently and then levels out before bending left to eventually arrive at a lane, also the Icknield Way (see "Taming the Lions").

Cross the lane and join a narrow path the other side which leads through a kissing gate into a field. *The field is known locally as Cow Common and up until the second World War was open common. During the war it was used by the Government to grow crops and for a short time, it was also used as a nine hole golf course. Today, it is auctioned annually for grazing.* Go straight across the field, in the direction of a footpath sign pointing to Ewelme and on reaching the right hand perimeter, do not go over a stile but bear left instead to follow the field perimeter along the top of the valley. You should leave the field at the corner, passing through a kissing gate to do so, to arrive at a small parking area beside a playing field on your left. Walk through the parking area and turn left along a lane in the direction of a sign for Benson and Wallingford. Follow the lane past "Old Rectory Cottage" to arrive at the historic village ,of Ewelme.

Ewelme (OS. 646915 Map 175). *The entrance to Ewelme is a dramatic one. To the left is the imposing "Fords Farm" with its huge barns and beautiful orchard painting an idyllic picture of rural England. To the right towering above you, stands reputedly the oldest primary school in the country, its proud stone windows letting in light on over five hundred years of study.*

The name Ewelme, like the village, is ancient and means "river source". The source is still strong today and quickly forms a wide stream which has been dammed to cultivate watercress. The village pond, often still called King's Pond after King Henry VIII's fondness for bathing in it, dates from the earliest settlement and before Christianity, was an important sacred site. Water, long before Christianity set foot in England, was regarded as sacred. The Celts, in particular, believed gods lived near springs and in rivers and would give up their most prized possessions, usually jewels and weaponry, to the water. This is one reason why so many important archeological finds are found in rivers. It is also the origin of the common practice of throwing coins into a fountain or wishing well.

Today, it is not the sacred pond that dominates the village but the magnificent 15th century school and alms houses. Together with the church, they are perhaps the best collection of 15th century buildings in England. The school was founded by Alice Chaucer and her husband William de la Pole, Earl of Suffolk. Alice Chaucer was the granddaughter of England's first recognised poet, Geoffrey Chaucer, author of "Canterbury Tales". On his death he was buried at Westminster Abbey in an area thereafter to be known as Poets Corner.

Geoffrey Chaucer's eldest son, Thomas (some historians doubt whether Thomas was Chaucer's son), went on to become Speaker of the House of Commons and later married the heiress of Ewelme. Their daughter, Alice, lived at Ewelme and put most of her efforts and much of her wealth into the village, making her very popular with local residents. The reliability of village life must have been sanctuary in what was to be, at times, an immensely tragic life. Her first marriage to Thomas Montagu, Earl of Salisbury, was short lived. In 1428, he led the Seige of Orleans in France only to be killed the following year defending an attack on the seige by an army led by Joan of Arc.

married a year later to another Earl, William de la Pole, Earl of Suffolk. In

1437, they set about remoulding the village to the scene we see today. First the church was started and after receiving a licence from Henry VI, work commenced on the alms houses and school. Their structure of brick (from Nettlebed), a method brought by the Earl from his native county, was unusual in this part of England and still stands out from the other buildings in the village today. There are thirteen alms houses and a master's house which encircle a small courtyard. Since the reign of James I, the master has been the Regius Professor of Medicine at Oxford and to this day, the professor and his family still regularly use the house. At the centre of the courtyard is a well with a cast iron wheel, which once gave the elderly inhabitants easy access to fresh water. You are welcome to look around the alms houses, but please respect their residents. Peering through a window will not bring a welcome response. The school has seen uninterrupted education since the day it was built, the forty children who attend today still wear the traditional school uniform.

Alice's marriage to William was also to end in tragedy. In 1449, William was made a Duke, the Duke of Suffolk, and one of his hardest duties was to oversee the troubled English territories in France. In the same year, the French exasperated in their attempts to win back their land through negotiation, invaded Normandy. The result, in England, was a rebellion by the people, led by one Jack Cade. The King and the English Government fled. The Duke of Suffolk made for exile in Flanders. The more unruly of the rebels learned of his plans and intercepted his vessel in the Channel near Dover. His captors brutally murdered the Duke and then beheaded him in a mock execution before throwing his body into the sea. One can only begin to imagine Alice's fear and grief during these tragic times. She never remarried but instead found solace in her beloved Ewelme, where she lived until her death twentyfive years later.

The manor remained in the Suffolk family until 1487 when it was confiscated by Henry VII for Alice's eldest grandson's part in a rebellion against him. Tragedy and bad luck continued to dog the Suffolks. In 1513, Edmund, Earl of Suffolk, was executed by Henry VIII and just twelve years later, the family came to a sudden end when the last heir, Richard, was killed at the Battle of Pavia.

After confiscating the house, Henry VII replaced the building with a palace. His son, Henry VIII, later spent his honeymoon with Catherine Howard here and Elizabeth I spent her childhood at the palace. The "Mad Cavalier", Prince Rupert, a Commander under Charles I, also stayed at the palace during the Civil War. At the end of the Civil War, the palace was abandoned and fell into ruin. Its site is now occupied by the current manor house.

The village church which watches over the village from a high prospect on the valley side, has a number of fitting memorials to the people who have shaped the village's past. Appropriately, the finest of these is a large richly decorated alabaster tomb of Alice, Duchess of Suffolk. Another memorial on the north wall of the chancel remembers Francis Martyn. We must say a special thanks to this man for it was his gallant action which saved the church from almost certain depredation. Francis Martyn, a Ewelme man, was a Colonel in Cromwell's army during the Civil War. Ewelme saw occupation by both the Royalist and Parliamentarian armies and it was during the occupation of the latter, that the church was threatened with plunder. Cromwell's troups systematically went from church to church mindlessly destroying memorials associated with England's royal heritage. At Ewelme, their Commander, Francis Martyn, locked the church door and stood at the entrance against his own soldiers, thus saving the church to be appreciated by future generations.

There are many more fine memorials and there is an excellent guide to their history for sale in the church. Perhaps one other worth a mention is in the churchyard where on the path to the old rectory there lies a headstone to the grave of Jerome K. Jerome, author of "Three Men in a Boat". Probably the best view of the village is gained from the churchyard, from where you can fully appreciate the splendour of the church, school and alms houses together. Undamaged through a turbulent history, they remain the biggest and best memorial to the piety of their founder, Alice Chaucer.

After passing between the famous school on your right and "Fords Farm" on the left, you will meet another lane. Follow this ahead to almost immediately after, turn right onto a narrow lane which leads gently uphill. If however, you are in need of refreshments then by making a short detour (one mile) by continuing ahead, you can visit "The Sheperds Hut", Morland. (To do this, on reaching the village pond take a lane ahead to your left and follow it until you arrive at the pub. You will have to retrace your steps to rejoin our walk). There is also a general stores opposite the village pond.

Returning to our route, follow the narrow lane uphill passing a number of picturesque cottages, where near the top it narrows to become no more than a path and shortly after, forks. You should take the right hand fork to arrive at a lane beside the entrance to the church. Turn right along the lane and ignore a signposted footpath off to the left. Pass the church and "The Old Rectory" and then leave the lane to join a track on the left, signposted as a public footpath. As the track bends left to service a house, leave it to carry straight on along a path passing to the left of some allotments. The path continues to shortly enter a field which you should cross, heading for a stile the other side. At this point you have good views ahead to Ewelme and Swyncombe Down and behind, to the cooling towers of Didcot Power Station.

At the far side of the field go over the stile into another field and bear gently diagonally left across the centre, again heading for a stile visible at the far side. Go over the stile into a third field and cross it, maintaining the same direction. Half way across the field just before the path descends, there are superb panoramic views of the surrounding countryside and Chiltern escarpment. After pausing to appreciate the views, descend to meet a stile at the far left hand corner which you should cross to arrive at a lane.

Turn left along the lane which follows the route of the ancient Icknield Way, at this point traversing an area known locally as Warren Bottom. Sometime later, ignore a signposted Right of Way off to your left and continue to follow the lane, ignoring a bridleway further on off to the right (also the Swan's Way). When the lane eventually bends sharp right in front of some woodland, you should leave it to take a track ahead which is marked as a bridleway as well as the Swan's Way. Soon after, ignore a crossing track and carry straight on with the wood on your right. You are now following both the Swan's Way and the Icknield Way. If the track is very muddy, it is possible to take a path running parallel with the track in the wood.

The woodland eventually ends and here you have a choice. The official route carries straight on. However, if you wish to take a short cut or make a short detour to visit Swyncombe Down from where the best views on the walk are obtained, continue as follows.

Short cut/detour - *Before starting, I must stress that this route is not a public right way and although the path is frequently used by the public, Swyncombe Down* *remains private property. As the wood ends, leave the track by taking a path right to pass beside a metal gate to thereafter, continue ahead along the path following the line of a field on your left. The path takes you to the top of Swyncombe Down where you gain the best views on the walk. You can now either retrace your steps from here or continue to follow the path which runs parallel with a bank, an ancient earth work, to rejoin the route by turning right onto the Ridgeway path at grid reference* **OS. 683914.**

Returning to the official route, continue ahead ignoring a track off to the left soon after. The track you are on now runs between fields where there are views left across to "Britwell Salome House". *Built in 1728, the house is the seat of the Simeon family. The stone column in front of the house was erected in 1764 by Sir Edward Simeon in memory of his parents.* Later, the track bends right and you gain yet more good views left to Beacon Hill and the National Trust owned Watlington Hill. The tall lone mast behind it marks Christmas Common, featured on "The Christmas Cracker". There are also two aerial masts ahead which are for Police communications.

The track soon bends left and descends to meet the Ridgeway (signposted). Turn right here onto the Ridgeway, pass through a metal gate and keep left passing the farm buildings of "North Farm". After the farm the track runs between a field on your right and a strip of woodland on the left, heading for Swyncombe Down. The Ridgeway soon begins to climb and later meets another track where you should turn right in the direction of a yellow arrow and white acorn, thereby continuing your ascent of Swyncombe Down.

The Ridgeway now enters woodland (where the short cut over Swyncombe Down now rejoins our official route - Grid ref. **OS. 683914**), and twists before going over the top of the down. As the track begins to descend the other side, you should ignore a turning left and keep to the main track ahead which now descends quite steeply. You should ignore all further turnings off to the left and right and continue to follow the main track in the direction of the yellow arrows and white acorns, to eventually arrive at a large field which traverses a deep valley. Unfortunately, the valley cannot be avoided and you should therefore, continue ahead along the right hand field perimeter, descending to the valley bottom and up the other side.

At the far side of the field go over a stile beside a gate, cross a lane and join a road opposite signposted to the church of St. Botolph and Swycombe (also marked as the Ridgeway). After passing to the right of "The Rectory", the road descends and bends right to become a track before arriving at St. Botolph church.

The Church of St. Botolph, Swyncombe (OS. 683902 Map 175) *is an idyllic Norman church, simplicity being the key to its beauty. The settlement which the church once served has long gone, though the manor house still remains, even though it is of modern construction.*

Milo Crispin, an early Norman owner of Swyncombe, gave the estate to the Abbey of Bec in Normandy. King John later granted the monks the right to hold an annual fair at Swyncombe, in those days a valuable source of income. The fair was held for five consecutive days around St. Botolph's Day, 17th June. Over the centuries, the dates were changed according to the politics of the day and the fair was eventually stopped in the 19th century. Today, it is hard to imagine a boistrous fair ever to place in this tranquil setting.

Pass through a gate on your left to enter the churchyard and follow the path round to the front of the church. From the church porch follow the path which is lined by neatly cut yews, downhill and exit via a gate the other side. Take time to look back here and note in particular, the tiny sheltered bell beside the church porch. After leaving the churchyard, turn left along a grass path which shortly forks and take the left hand fork, though do not take the path on the immediate left which follows the perimeter of the churchyard, to immediately after, cross a drive. Carry straight on, following a wooden fence on your left, to pass through a kissing gate into a field.

Continue ahead, going uphill across the centre of the field where several carefully planted beech trees provide an excellent example of well-managed estate land. As you progress, there are good views behind to your right of "Swyncombe House" with the unusual but not unsightly backdrop of Didcot Power Station. At the far side of the field after taking in the views (your final view of Didcot), pass through a kissing gate and follow a path uphill through Church Wood, ignoring another path off to the right as you begin. Later, go over a crossing track and continue ahead along a track the other side which soon levels out and continues in a straight line through the centre of the wood. Eventually, You will arrive at the other side of the wood where you should go over a stile and turn right along a lane, heading for the village of Cookley Green.

As you arrive at the village green the lane you have been following bends right and another lane joins from the left. You should leave the lane at this point and continue straight ahead across the left hand edge of the green and to the right of a line of scots pines. To your right you will see the village war memorial. Cookley Green is a relatively modern village and apart from farming, grew from the need for servants at "Swyncombe House".

At the far side of the green you will meet the B481 for the second time today, which you should cross to then turn left along the grass verge the other side. After a few paces, turn right onto a track marked as a no through road. Follow the track, passing a number of lovely properties, the last being "Stockings Farm Cottage". The name does not refer to the silk variety, but is derived from the Saxon word "stoccing" meaning "tree stumps". After the cottage, maintain your route ahead and ignore a path off to the left. The track is bordered by banks and ancient hedgerows, a sign of its having been here for centuries - it is interesting to contemplate the many walks of life that have used this route over the years. It slowly descends passing through an area of scrub, a mass of bluebells in spring, and later narrows to become a path. Thereafter, it eventually meets a prominent path which leads up the valley side to your left (not part of our route) to Russells Water which boasts the highest pond in the Chilterns.

Our route is straight on, not left, continuing a slow descent following the valley floor. As you progress, ignore a path off to the right marked as footpath "SW15", and carry straight on to later arrive at a small beech copse on your right. Ignore more marked footpaths (white arrows) off to the left and right and continue ahead where your route becomes bordered by wooden fencing, passing to the left of the beech copse before continuing between fields. Ahead now is the welcome sight of woodland belonging to Warburg Nature Reserve.

The path as you have progressed has widened gradually and after the beech copse becomes a track. Further on, the track forks in front of a public footpath sign, where you should take the left hand fork, heading for the woodland of Warburg Nature

Reserve (do not make the mistake of taking the footpath on your left here). It is not long before you are greeted by a BBONT nature reserve sign and you should continue ahead along the track through the carefully managed woodland of the reserve. One word of warning however, do not relax too soon thinking that it is only a few paces back to our starting point. As mentioned at the start of the walk, this is BBONT's largest nature reserve and it is still another mile to the finish.

Keep to the track, ignoring any turnings off, at one point going over a crossing track to eventually arrive back at the Visitors Centre and car park, our starting point. Unfortunately, there is not a pub here into which you can stagger to celebrate finishing the walk, but if you feel anything like I did at the end, perhaps you do not have the energy to lift a glass anyway!

ACCOMMODATION
The White Hart Hotel, Nettlebed. Tel: 0491 641245
On the walk, this is a luxurious traditional old coaching inn with plenty of character. In the evening you need go no further to retain the historical atmosphere of the walk.

Fords Farm, Ewelme. Tel: 0491 839272
On the walk, Fords Farm gives you the experience of living on one of the most beautiful farms in the Chilterns with the added attraction of staying in the centre of a truly historic village.

Camping and Caravanning, Black Horse Farm, Checkendon. Tel: 0491 680418
Approximately four miles from the walk, this is a lovely small and secluded site opposite one of the few remaining truly traditional pubs in the Chilterns. The site is open to Camping and Caravanning Club members only. For details of membership, tel: 0203 694995.